W9-BLS-233

THE INNER STRUCTURE OF TAI CHI

Tai Chi Chi Kung I

Mantak Chia & Juan Li

Preface by
Jampa Mackenzie Stewart

Illustrated by
Juan Li & Michael Abbey

General Editor: Jampa Mackenzie Stewart

Copy Editor: Judith Stein

Editorial Assistance Dennis Lewis

Contributing Writers: Jampa Mackenzie Stewart,
Kimberly Baldt, Gary Oshinsky

Illustrations: Juan Li & Michael Abbey (Chapter 4)

Coordination: Lynnette Brooks

Design and Production: MG Manelis,
                      Madison Southwest
                      with JM Stewart & L Brooks

© 1996, Mantak and Maneewan Chia

First published in 1996 by:
Healing Tao Books
PO Box 1194
Huntington, NY 11743

ISBN: 0-935621-50-4
Library of Congress Catalog Number: 95-082138

Manufactured in the United States of America
First Printing, 1996

10 9 8 7 6 5 4 3 2

All rights reserved. No part of this book may be used or reproduce in any
manner whatsoever without the express written permission from the
author. With exception of brief quotations embodied in critical articles and
reviews.

Dedicated to
Tai Chi Practitioners
Everywhere

Table of Contents

About the Authors

Mantak & Maneewan Chia

MASTER MANTAK CHIA

Master Mantak Chia is the creator of the Healing Tao system and the director of Tao Gardens in the beautiful northern country of Thailand. Since childhood he has been studying the Taoist approach to life as well. His mastery of this ancient knowledge, enhanced by his study of other disciplines, has resulted in the development of the Healing Tao System which is now being taught throughout the world.

Mantak Chia was born in Thailand to Chinese parents in 1944. When he was six years old, Buddhist monks taught him how to sit and "still the mind." While still a grammar school student, he first learned traditional Thai boxing. He then was taught Tai Chi Chuan by Master Lu, who soon introduced him to Aikido, Yoga, and broader levels of Tai Chi.

Years later, when he was a student in Hong Kong excelling in track and field events, a senior classmate named Cheng Sue-sue introduced him to his first esoteric teacher and Taoist Master, Master Yi Eng (I Yun). At this point, Master Chia began his studies of the Taoist way of life in earnest. He learned how to circulate energy through the Microcosmic Orbit, and, through the practice of Fusion of the Five Elements, how to open the other Six Special Channels. As he further studied Inner Alchemy, he learned the Enlightenment of the Kan and Li, Sealing of the Five Sense Organs, Congress of Heaven and Earth, and Reunion of Heaven and Man. It was Master Yi Eng who authorized Master Chia to teach and heal.

In his early twenties Mantak Chia studied with Master Meugi in Singapore, who taught him Kundalini, Taoist yoga and the Buddhist Palm. He was soon able to clear blockages to the flow of energy within his own body. He also learned to pass life force energy through his hands to heal the patients of Master Meugi. He then learned Chi Nei Tsang from Dr. Mui Yimwattana in Thailand.

Later, he studied with Master Cheng Yao-Lun who taught him the Shao-Lin Method of Internal Power. He also learned from Master Yao-Lun the closely guarded secret of the organs, glands and bone marrow exercise known as *Bone Marrow Nei Kung* and the exercise know as *Strengthening and Renewal of the Tendons*. Master Cheng Yao-Lun's system combined Thai boxing and Kung Fu. At this time Master Chia also studied with Master Pan Yu, whose system combined Taoist, Buddhist and Zen teachings. From master Pan Yu he learned about the exchange of Yin and Yang power between men and women, and also learned how to develop the *Steel Body*.

To understand the mechanisms behind healing energy better, Master Chia studied Western anatomy and medical science for two years. While pursuing his studies, he managed the Gestetner Company, a manufacturer of office equipment, and became well acquainted with the technology of offset printing and copying machines.

Using his knowledge of Taoism combined with the other disciplines, Master Chia began teaching the Healing Tao System. he eventually trained other teachers to communicate this knowledge, and he established the Natural Healing Center in Thailand. Five years later, he decided to move to New York where, in 1979, he opened the Healing Tao Center. During his years in America, Master Chia continued his studies in the Wu system of Tai Chi with Edward Yee in New York.

Since then, Master Chia has taught tens of thousands of students throughout the world, and has trained nearly 200 certified instructors to propagate his system. Healing Tao centers have opened up in many locations, including Boston, Philadelphia, Denver, Chicago, San Francisco, Los Angeles, San Diego, Houston, Tucson, Santa Fe and Toronto. Groups have also formed in England, Germany, the Netherlands, Italy, France, Switzerland, Austria, India, Australia, Japan and Thailand.

In 1994, Master Chia and his family moved back to Thailand, where they had begun construction of Tao Gardens, an international Healing Tao retreat center in Chiang Mai. Today he lives there with his wife, Maneewan, and their teenage son, Max (In 1990 Max, at age 11, became the youngest certified instructor in the Healing Tao System).

Master Chia is a warm, friendly and helpful man who views himself primarily as a teacher. He presents the Healing Tao in a straightforward and practical manner while always expanding his knowledge and approach to teaching. He uses a word processor for writing and is very much at ease with the latest computer technology.

He has previously written and published ten Healing Tao books: in 1983, *Awaken Healing Energy of the Tao*; in 1984, *Taoist Secrets of Love: Cultivating Male Sexual Energy*; in 1985, *Taoist Ways to Transform Stress into Vitality*; in 1986, *Chi Self-Massage: The Tao of Rejuvenation* and *Iron Shirt Chi Kung I*; and *Healing Love Through the Tao: Cultivating Female Sexual Energy*; in 1989, *Bone Marrow Nei Kung*; in 1990, *Fusion of the Five Elements I* and *Chi Nei Tsang: Internal Organ Chi Massage*; and in 1993, *Awaken Healing Light of the Tao*.

Master Chia estimates that it will take twenty books to convey the full Healing Tao System. In June, 1990 at a dinner in San Francisco, Master Chia was honored by the International Congress of Chinese Medicine and Qi Gong (Chi Kung), who named him the Qi gong Master of the Year. He is the first recipient of this annual award.

JUAN LI

Juan Li was born in 1946 in Havana, Cuba. He began his Taoist studies in 1965 with a comparative study of the *Tao Te Ching* in English translations. He went on to major in Chinese studies at Brooklyn College, where he specialized in Chinese history of the Shang and Chou dynasties. At this time he also began a special research and study project on the I Ching, a subject with which he is still deeply involved.

His first Tai Chi training took place in San Francisco with Sifu Sik Ho Chu, who introduced him to the Fu style of Tai Chi, a form developed in Honan province during the 19th century by Fu Juen Ko. Fu style is characterized by the use of extremely graceful hand movements and low stances for greater power. After teaching Fu style, Sifu Sik Ho Chu introduced Juan Li to Wu style Tai Chi and the Liang Yee form of Kung Fu.

In 1982 Juan Li met Master Mantak Chia for the first time, and began his study of the traditional Taoist internal energy formulas. Soon after their meeting, Juan Li began helping with the illustrations of Master Chia's books. Master Chia also introduced him to the 13 movement form of Yang style and the Wu style broad sword form.

Eventually Juan Li went on to become a senior instructor in the Healing Tao System, and today he spends the greater part of his time presenting these teachings in Western Europe. Juan Li lives in Santa Fe, New Mexico with his wife, Renu, who is also a senior Healing Tao Instructor.

Preface

DR. JAMPA MACKENZIE STEWART

When I first met Master Mantak Chia in 1982, I had practiced and taught Tai Chi for about ten years. I had already learned Old Chen style, Yang style, Wu style, Cheng Man-Ching style, and Twenty-Four style Tai Chi. In fact, I knew so many different Tai Chi forms that I could not practice them all in one day.

For years I had read books about the mysterious inner changes that were supposed to take place as a result of Tai Chi practice—transforming sexual energy into Chi and Chi into spirit. Yet the Tai Chi teachers I studied with either didn't know about these practices or wouldn't divulge their knowledge. While I practiced hard what I had been taught, I was frustrated by the snail's pace at which I seemed to be progressing. I was elated to finally find Mantak Chia, a true Taoist master who was openly teaching the esoteric secrets of Taoist Inner Alchemy.

Still, the last thing I wanted to learn was another Tai Chi form! When I first saw Master Chia's Tai Chi Chi Kung form, there seemed to be nothing to it — only Grasping the Bird's Tail and Single Whip. I already knew five different ways of doing these movements. I was therefore able to learn Master Chia's form in one day. Or so I thought.

I was quite proud of my Tai Chi when I went to the Catskill Mountains in upstate New York for Master Chia's teacher training retreat in the summer of 1986. Master Chia required that all his instructors learn Tai Chi Chi Kung as a prerequisite for teaching the higher-level practices of the Healing Tao. "No sweat," I thought. "My years of prior training will stand me in good stead."

What a rude and humiliating awakening I was in for! Master Chia was merciless with me, and brutally frank in his assessment of my Tai Chi. "You barely passed," he told me. "How can you practice Tai Chi for so many years and still have no root?" Each successive year thereafter, he would say to me, "You still don't get it! No spinal cord power. No spiraling. If you teach Tai Chi, you have to know these things." How could there be so much to master in so short a form?

It slowly dawned on me, through the veils of my stubborn pride and tenacious ignorance, that Tai Chi has nothing to do with the number of moves one learns or the different styles one knows; it's the quality of each movement that counts. If one understands the profound principles of body mechanics, energy transfer, and mental focus that have been preserved within Tai Chi from the earliest masters down to the present, then everything one does is Tai Chi. On the other hand, if one doesn't grasp the principles of inner structure, then although one's Tai Chi movements may look beautiful, one's form is empty and hollow.

Western boxing has only about five techniques, yet consider how difficult is to become a champion boxer like Muhammed Ali or Mike Tyson. Tai Chi has thirteen basic techniques, as well as hundreds of inner principles of movement. The simple form of Tai Chi Chi Kung contains them all.

With fewer outer movements to perform, the Tai Chi Chi Kung student quickly progresses from the initial stage of learning the outer form to the stage of mastering the inner structure of Tai Chi. I had to begrudgingly admit that Master Chia's students, who had studied Tai Chi Chi Kung with him for only three intensive weeks, were further along than my students who had studied the longer Tai Chi forms over two or three years!

Most other traditional Tai Chi masters required their students to train in Tai Chi for years before they exposed them to internal energy work such as the Microcosmic Orbit Meditation. After years of devoted study and service, the master would secretly take the fortunate and diligent student into his inner sanctum and reward him by teaching him the Microcosmic Orbit as the crowning initiation in his training.

Part of Master Chia's genius is his insistence that students learn the Microcosmic Orbit Meditation and Iron Shirt Chi Kung at the outset as prerequisites to Tai Chi Chi Kung. Master Chia teaches Tai Chi as one limb of the Healing Tao system, an integrated approach to cultivating healing energy through the Tao. All the different parts of the Healing Tao system—sitting meditation, standing meditation, moving meditation, cultivation of sexual energy, and healing work—mutually support one another. One's progress in meditation, healing, and Chi Kung—internal energy work—is immediately reflected in one's Tai Chi, and vice-versa.

Tai Chi Chi Kung teaches one to move in harmony with the principles of the Tao. It is based on classical Taoist philosophy as presented in the *I Ching*; in the *Tao Te Ching*; in Chuang Tzu and Lieh Tzu; and in Sun Tzu's *The Art of War*. Its principles are also rooted in the esoteric Taoist teachings of Inner Alchemy as taught by the great immortals Ko Hung, Lu Tung-Pin, and others. The legends say it was a Taoist immortal, Chang San-Feng of Wu Tang Mountain, who originally created Tai Chi. More modern historical research seems to indicate it was probably a retired Ming Dynasty general, Chen Wang-Ting, who developed Tai Chi and taught it to the people of his village as their clan's martial arts style. In any event, Chen's writings clearly show that he too was deeply steeped in esoteric Taoist Inner Alchemy.

Knowledge is power. In the days when warfare meant hand-to-hand combat, martial arts skills were military secrets and were not taught openly. Similarly, the esoteric methods of Taoist internal alchemical cultivation were reserved for selected and carefully screened initiates. Even in this century, that tradition of secrecy has continued to a great extent. Contemporary Tai Chi masters still have their exoteric students and their select "indoor" disciples who receive the full transmission of the art. The Chinese are so good at keeping secrets that the outer students often don't even know what they are missing.

Fortunately, this pattern seems to be changing. Through the openness of Master Chia and other recent masters, the proverbial cat is out of the bag. The teachings are now available for whoever wants to take advantage of this golden opportunity to receive the sublime distillation of thousands of years of Chinese wisdom.

This book presents the first levels of the art of Tai Chi Chi Kung. Master Chia calls his form *Tai Chi Chi Kung*, instead of the usual name, *Tai Chi Chuan*. *Chuan* literally means *fist* and denotes an emphasis on the use of the art for fighting. *Chi Kung* means *energy cultivation*. While Chi Kung can be applied toward enhancing one's martial arts abilities, it can also be directed toward healing oneself and others, or toward refining one's spirit for the realization of wisdom and inner peace.

Although martial skills are certainly a significant part of Master Chia's presentation of Tai Chi Chi Kung, in the hierarchy of importance the ability to defend oneself and secure a peaceful environment ought to be followed by the wise use of the life force one has fought to preserve. A life dedicated only to fighting seems tragic, does it not? Learning to heal oneself and then to heal others, learning to soar into the realms of the spirit, returning to harmony with oneself, with society, and with nature, are what we are really here to do.

Jampa Mackenzie Stewart is a general editor of Healing Tao Books and a Senior Healing Tao Instructor. He was the major contributing writer for *Awaken Healing Light of the Tao* (Healing Tao Books, 1993), and is the author of *The Life of Gampopa: The Incomparable Dharma Lord of Tibet* (Snow Lion Publications, 1995), and *Foundations of Taoist Practice* (1995).

He has also published over forty articles on Tai Chi, Taoist meditation, Chi Kung, and healing for numerous periodicals and professional journals. He is the former publisher and editor of *The Tai Chi Journal*, an international Tai Chi magazine, and the former director of the Rochester Tai Chi Chuan Center in Rochester, New York.

Mackenzie is also a Doctor of Oriental Medicine and a practicing acupuncturist. He currently teaches classes and workshops in the Healing Tao throughout the United States and holds regular Tai Chi and Healing Tao programs and retreats in the high desert country of New Mexico.

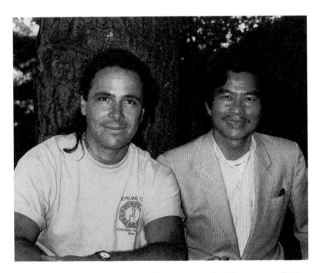

Jampa Mackenzie Stewart & Master Chia

Foreword

Mantak Chia

The form described in this book is called Tai Chi Chi Kung. I have now studied and practiced Tai Chi for more than thirty years. I began by learning three different forms of Yang style Tai Chi from five different masters. Later I learned Wu style, with Master Edward Yee, and then Chen style Tai Chi. Finally, I met Master P.Y. Tam, who taught me Tai Chi Chi Kung, a very early form of the Yang style, emphasizing the use of the mind and heart to move Chi. The Chi in turn improves the circulation, enlivens the bone structure, and revitalizes the whole system.

The Tai Chi Chi Kung form stresses the inner structure of Tai Chi, the way Chi flows in the body, and the way energy is transmitted through the bone structure from the ground. This form is simple and easy to master, yet it contains all the essential movements of Tai Chi.

In the past, most masters have taught 108-movement forms of Tai Chi, making the learning process extremely complicated and time consuming. In many cases it took years simply to learn the form before the students could begin to explore the inner structure of Tai Chi. Using this short and essential Tai Chi Chi Kung form, the student can almost immediately begin to apply the vital principles of Tai Chi: absorbing, transforming, and directing the three forces. The three forces are the Universal force, which comes from the stars, sun, and moon; the Cosmic force, which comes from the cosmic particles in and around the atmosphere and environment; and the Earth energy, which comes from the earth itself.

The Tai Chi principles and methods of internal power training are applicable to all styles of Tai Chi. However, Tai Chi Chi Kung must be understood, studied, and practiced within the context of Taoism; it is but one branch (albeit an important one) of a comprehensive system of Taoist practices. Each branch relies on the other branches for support. In this book there are thus numerous references to the Taoist meditations and Chi Kung practices that I teach my Tai Chi students within the context of the Healing Tao system. I have already written many books describing these practices in minute and complete detail, so readers wishing in-depth information should refer to these works. However, I have also included brief descriptions of the beginning level Healing Tao practices both in the main text and in the appendices for the benefit of new readers and students.

We wish you every success in your study and mastery of Tai Chi Chi Kung. May the Chi be with you!

Mantak Chia
Chiang Mai, Thailand, 1995

Acknowledgements

We extend our gratitude to the many generations of Taoist and Tai Chi masters who have passed on their special lineage as an unbroken oral transmission over thousands of years. We particularly thank Taoist Master I Yun (Yi Eng) for his openness in transmitting the formulas of Taoist Inner Alchemy, Wu style Tai Chi Master Edward Yee who taught me the complete Tai Chi system, Tai Chi Master P.Y. Tam for the teaching of Tai Chi Chi Kung, and Master Cheng Yao-Lun for his teachings of Changing the Tendons and Sinews and Washing the Bone Marrow.

We offer our eternal gratitude to our parents and teachers for their many gifts to us. Remembering them brings joy and satisfaction to our continued efforts in presenting the Healing Tao system.

We express our special thanks to Juan Li for his fine illustrations and for his preparation of the original draft of the first half of the manuscript. As always, he has played an integral role in presenting the Healing Tao concepts and techniques.

We express our deep appreciation to Jampa Mackenzie Stewart for his overall help in organizing and editing this book, for his writing contributions, for his book design, and for his assistance and guidance throughout its entire preparation.

Special thanks also to Judith Stein for her editorial guidance with the final text.

We thank Kimberly Baldt for her editing and transcribing the second part of the manuscript. We thank Dennis Lewis for his excellent and generous editorial and production advice.

We thank Gary Oshinsky for his editing and writing contributions during the later stages of preparation. Many thanks also to Karl Danskin for videotaping the Tai Chi Chi Kung demonstrations and teachings on the advanced levels of practice.

Special thanks to Lynnette Brooks for her layout assistance, contributions, and general assistance during the completion phases of the book.

We are also grateful to Michael Manelis for his computer graphic skills, cover design, and design and production of the book.

Finally, we wish to thank our Certified Instructors, students, and sponsors throughout the world for their ongoing contributions to the system and for preserving the vitality of the Healing Tao practices.

Words of Caution

The practices described in this book have been used successfully for hundreds of years by Taoists and Tai Chi practitioners trained by personal instruction. Readers should not undertake the practice of Tai Chi Chi Kung without personal training by the Healing Tao since certain of these practices, if improperly done, may cause injury or result in health problems. This book is intended to supplement individual training by the Healing Tao and to serve as a reference guide for these practices. Anyone who undertakes these practices on the basis of this book alone does so entirely at his or her own risk.

The practices described herein are NOT intended to be used as a substitute for professional medical care. If any readers are suffering from illnesses based on mental or emotional disorders, an appropriate professional health care practitioner or therapist should be consulted. Such problems should be corrected before you start training.

Neither the Healing Tao nor its staff and instructors can be responsible for the consequences of any practice or misuse of the information contained in this book. If the reader undertakes any exercise without strictly following the instructions, notes and warnings, the responsibility must lie solely with the reader.

Part One

Introduction

China's oldest system of philosophy and spiritual practice is Taoism. Taoists observe that we are part of nature; we are born of the energy of the earth and stars and elements. Yet, for some reason, we forget our place in nature, and so we need to learn how to reclaim our rightful heritage as children of nature.

The way of nature is called the Tao. The way to realizing our highest potential, living in harmony with the patterns and energy of nature, is also called the Tao. To Taoists, the journey and the goal are one. Life is lived as a process, as a dance.

Just as the universe is an integrated whole, the body is an integrated whole, with each part connected to and dependent on the other parts. Yet as we become adults leading sedentary lives, we often forget to use all the parts of our bodies. We depend on the head and arms, using the spine, hips, and legs only to get us from the car to the elevator to the swivel seat, where we can use the head and arms again. By restricting our movement, we forget how to move strongly, lithely, and efficiently. When we forget how to live fully in our bodies, we overly restrict the way we move, and eventually we forget who we really are.

Tai Chi Chi Kung is an integral part of Taoism. Based on the highest principles of the Tao, it is both an expression of the Tao through movement and a personal practice for understanding and realizing the essence of the Tao. Through daily Tai Chi Chi Kung practice, we can become as children again, without stiffness or tension. We can relearn to move freely and naturally with the whole body connected, both structurally and energetically. In this way, we mirror our connection to the larger whole, as part of the universe. Through Tai Chi Chi Kung, we can become fully ourselves.

There are many styles of Tai Chi today. Regardless of style, the first step is to learn and remember the outer movements. When one practices all the movements in sequence, that is called the Tai Chi form. Once one learns the form, the rest of the work in mastering Tai Chi involves learning to use energy in each posture. Working with Chi or energy is called *internal work*.

The internal work is what makes Tai Chi unique and what distinguishes it from the external forms of martial arts. The inner structure is what allows the body to move as a whole. Not learning the internal part of Tai Chi is like never bothering to look inside the oyster to find the pearl.

The foundation of mastering the internal structure of Tai Chi is energy meditation. Many Tai Chi students around the world do not receive any training in energy meditation; unfortunately, most people are taught long and difficult Tai Chi forms first. To learn the form, they have to go through many years of practice and correction to perfect the outer form and make it look beautiful. Because of the time devoted to the outer form, the internal work is often neglected.

The major advantage of Tai Chi Chi Kung is that it is a short form of thirteen movements, repeated in four directions. Although it is a short form, it contains the essence of the movements of the longer Tai Chi forms. Since it is repetitive, it does not take long to learn, so one can quickly proceed to the internal work. Once one becomes familiar with the essence of Tai Chi Chi Kung, learning the long forms is relatively easy.

Lack of meditation experience, along with the need to learn lengthy forms, makes it difficult for people to go into internal work. In the Healing Tao, these aspects of Tai Chi are taught separately as sitting energy meditation, standing meditation, and moving meditation.

Sitting Energy Meditation

The Lung Sound

In sitting meditation, the practitioner sits in a comfortable position. Through sitting practice one can strengthen one's awareness and concentration without being distracted by the body's movement. The first emphasis in this practice is to learn to quiet and focus the mind, and to relax the internal organs and other specific parts of the body. This phase is accomplished through the Inner Smile and the Six Healing Sounds.

The next step is to connect with life energy. One does this through the Microcosmic Orbit and the Fusion of the Five Elements meditations, wherein one trains the mind to feel Chi, to generate and gather it into a desired energy center, Tan Tien, to direct Chi to other areas for healing and strengthening, and then to store it for future use. Additionally, through a purification process, the energy is transformed to a higher level of mental quietness, balance, and inner happiness. If one learns Tai Chi without any sitting meditation, it is more difficult to feel Chi and to use the mind's eye to gather, concentrate, and guide the energy.

The Governing Channel

The Functional Channel

Pai-Hui (Crown)

Pituitary Gland (Mid-eyebrow)

Yu Chen (Cranial Pump)

Hsuan Chi (Throat Center)

Ta-Chui (C-7)

Shan Chung (Thymus Gland) Rejuvenation Center

Shen Tao (Opposite the Heart Center)

Chung Wan (Solar Plexus, Pancreas)

Chi Chung (Adrenal Gland Center at T-11; Mini Pump)

Shen Que (Navel, Spleen)

Ming Men (Kidney Point; Door of Life)

Kuan Yuan (Ovarian Palace) Jing Gong (Sperm Palace)

Tan Tien

Heding Extra-31

Chang Chiang, Coccyx (Sacral Pump)

Wei Chung BL-40 (extra spirit energy is stored here)

Hui Yin (Perineum; Gate of Death and Life)

The Microcosmic Orbit Pathway

Yung Chuan K-1

Standing Energy Meditation

After learning sitting meditation, one will find it easier to learn standing meditations such as Iron Shirt Chi Kung. In Iron Shirt Chi Kung, one gently packs or compresses energy and guides it through the Microcosmic Orbit. Additionally, one learns to adjust the structure of one's stance in alignment with gravity, so that one becomes "grounded" or "rooted" both structurally and energetically.

Once one has the feeling of aligning and integrating one's structure in this way while standing still, one can carry this experience into movement within the Tai Chi form. Standing meditation is the quickest and easiest way of mastering this vital internal aspect of Tai Chi. Nearly all the great Tai Chi masters acknowledge standing meditation as a major factor in their attainment of high levels of skill.

Moving Energy Meditation

Through Tai Chi Chi Kung, you can integrate what you have learned through sitting and standing meditation practice into movement. As you master the Tai Chi principles of movement, you can gradually apply these same principles in all your movements throughout daily life. Whether washing the dishes, doing yard work, or walking down the street, you will spontaneously move in harmony with the Tao. This is the essence of Tai Chi Chi Kung.

In this book, *The Inner Structure of Tai Chi: Tai Chi Chi Kung I*, you will first be introduced to the background, history, and basic principles of Tai Chi Chi Kung. Next, you will learn a set of simple yet powerful warm-up exercises to help open the energy centers, joints, and tendons. Following the warm-ups, you will learn to feel Chi through a simple standing energy meditation. After this, you will be guided step by step through the Tai Chi Chi Kung form.

Because the Tai Chi Chi Kung form consists of only thirteen easy-to-master movements, your mind is soon free to learn how to experience and direct the Chi flow.

Tai Chi is an art. As with most arts, personal instruction is essential if one wishes to reach the highest levels. This book has two main functions: to introduce beginners to the art of Tai Chi; and to help those who have already been practicing Tai Chi understand both the basic and the deeper underlying principles which many Tai Chi masters are unwilling to speak about. While this book can be used as a handbook by those already studying Tai Chi Chi Kung with a Certified Healing Tao Instructor, it will also be of great value to students of other Tai Chi styles, as the principles presented apply to all styles of Tai Chi.

Once you have learned the form, Chapter 6 presents different focuses for beginning and intermediate level practice. The rest of the book contains in-depth instruction for mastering the higher levels of all forms of Tai Chi.

If you do not have access to a Certified Healing Tao Instructor, you may find that having the Tai Chi Chi Kung I guided videocassette will be helpful in your practice at the beginning.

I
How Tai Chi Chi Kung Began: The History of Tai Chi and Its Place in the Healing Tao

THE ORIGINS OF TAI CHI CHI KUNG

Archeological discoveries during the last several decades have found ample evidence that calisthenics and breathing exercises were practiced as early as the Chou Dynasty (circa 1100-221 B.C.). Tai Chi probably developed out of ancient forms of Tao-In and Chi Kung exercise combined with internal circulation of energy and breath, and the popular martial applications of the time.

Traditional Tai Chi histories, written much later after Tai Chi had become widespread, state that during the fourteenth century a Taoist hermit by the name of Chang San-Feng received the Tai Chi teachings in a series of dreams. Other accounts assert that Chang San-Feng developed Tai Chi after observing a battle between a snake and a crane. Yet another version places Tai Chi's origins during the Tang Dynasty (618-907 A.D.).

Perhaps the most credible theory is that Tai Chi was created by Chen Wang-Ting, the ninth-generation chief of the Chen family clan in Honan province. Chen Wang-Ting was a general in the Ming Dynasty army. When the Ming Dynasty fell to the Manchurians in 1644,

Chen retired to Chenjiagou (Chen family village) in Honan province and used his military training to devise a series of movements to teach his clan members. The movements were based on the Red Fist style of the nearby Shaolin Temple, combined with movements from the famous boxing manual of General Chi Ji-Guang.

Some accounts say that years later, a wandering Taoist named Chuan Fa visited Chenjiagou and taught the Chen clan to adapt principles of the Tao (such as using the Chi flow and Yin and Yang) into their movements, thus converting the Chen family boxing into Tai Chi Chuan—the Supreme Ultimate Boxing. The Chen family, however, disputes these accounts, claiming Chuan Fa was merely a student of Chen Wang-Ting. The Chen family notes that it is clear from Chen Wang-Ting's early writings that he was already familiar with Taoist Inner Alchemy when he devised his Chen style Tai Chi forms. It is also clear that all the other common Tai Chi styles were later derived from Chen style Tai Chi.

Until the beginning of this century, Tai Chi was considered a secret practice, passed down within the closely knit structure of family and

Chang San-Feng, the legendary creator of Tai Chi.

with the Communist victory in 1949, martial arts made a slow transition from being a deadly art of war to becoming a health and longevity practice.

The last four decades in particular have witnessed the emergence of Tai Chi as a health practice among the masses of China. Visitors to China or any large overseas Chinese community regularly see large groups of people of all ages practicing Tai Chi outdoors in the early hours of the morning. The fascination with Tai Chi has also spread to non-Chinese communities all over the world. Before the Second World War began, the Asian martial arts were almost totally unknown in North America. It was during the war in the Pacific that American soldiers brought back news of the extraordinary abilities of some Japanese fighters.

During the occupation of Japan, many American soldiers began to study Judo, Jujitsu, Karate, and other Japanese martial arts. Soon after the Korean war, Korean martial arts were introduced to the West as well.

During the early sixties and mid-seventies, the predominant forms of martial arts practiced in North America and Europe were Judo, Karate, Aikido, and Tae Kwon Do. Tai Chi started to capture the public eye during the late sixties. Since then it has continued to spread, becoming one of the most widely practiced forms of health exercise all around the world.

The practice of Tai Chi, as popularized during this century, has come down to the present

loyal disciples. Training in the martial arts was very expensive to pursue. Accomplished masters would often demand exorbitant fees in gold bars, cash, or services. Morally, the masters expected total loyalty and obedience from the disciples. In addition, the training demanded many years of single-minded practice.

With the increasingly widespread availability and use of firearms, almost all the martial arts styles began a rapid decline. Because firearms required very little training and practically no discipline to master, those who learned to use a gun had a distinct advantage over those who had trained arduously in martial arts.

Thus the outlook seemed bleak for the martial arts at the dawn of this century. Faced with the prospect of their art becoming obsolete, some of the old masters began to teach openly to anyone who could afford it. As old Imperial China collapsed in chaos in 1912 and the experiment in a republican democracy ended

"Brush Knee and Twist Step" – Chen Family Style Tai Chi by Chen Fa-Kor (1887-1955), a 20th century descendant of the founder.

through three major family traditions. The first is the Chen family style, as described earlier, with its combination of soft and explosive power techniques. The second is the Yang family style, derived from the Chen style in the nineteenth century, with its smooth and

"Brush Knee and Twist Step" – Yang Family Style Tai Chi by Yang Cheng-Fu (1883-1936).

even-flowing tempo. The third is the Wu family style, derived from both the Chen and Yang forms in the nineteenth century, with its subtle joint movements.

"Brush Knee and Twist Step" – Wu Family Style Tai Chi by Wu Chien-Chuan (1870-1949).

Another famous but lesser-known family style is Sun style Tai Chi, a system created in the early twentieth century by the great internal style boxer Sun Lu-Tang, which combines elements of Hsing I Chuan and Pa Kua Chang within the Tai Chi sequence. Yet another lesser-known family system is Hao style Tai Chi, derived from Chen style in the nineteenth century and characterized by very small and

intricate circular movements. Still others include Fu style Tai Chi and Chen Pan-Ling style Tai Chi, both created in the twentieth century. These two are called combined styles because they integrate the flavor and expression of the three major family styles into their way of doing the movements.

There are also other non-family styles, some reputedly developed in the monasteries and temples centuries ago, and others created in this century. Some of these are Kuang Ping Tai Chi, Wu Tang Tai Chi, Yang's Twenty-Four style Tai Chi, and Cheng Man-Ching style (an abridged variation of the Yang family style).

THE TAI CHI CHI KUNG I THIRTEEN MOVEMENT FORM

The form we explore in this book is the thirteen-movement form, which we call Tai Chi Chi Kung I. This form is believed to have originated with the Chen family. In the nineteenth century, it was modified by the Yang family and passed down in numerous variations to the present.

Despite the multiplicity of styles and variations, the basic principles of all forms of Tai Chi are essentially the same:

1. Concentrating the mind and Chi.
2. Relaxing in movement while distinguishing the full (Yang) from the empty (Yin).
3. Keeping the body rooted to the ground and the center of gravity low.
4. Keeping the bone structure aligned with the forces of Heaven and Earth, and transferring the Earth force through the bone structure into a single point of discharge.
5. Allowing the Chi to circulate and move the muscles, bones, and tendons in slow, coordinated movements without ever pushing the physical limitations of the body to extremes, and moving smoothly and continuously with total bodily integration.

The thirteen-movement style is simple in its structure, yet it encompasses the essence of Tai Chi. The form is compact enough to be practiced in a space only four feet square. Tai

Chi Chi Kung is practiced to the four directions, starting with the north corner and moving counterclockwise, leading with the left hand; then returning clockwise, leading with the right hand. Because the right-side and left-side form follow each other, the Tai Chi set can be extended for as long as one desires. If time is limited, one can simply do the thirteen movements in just one direction.

Urban Tai Chi practitioners are often frustrated by the need to find a large private space for practicing the longer forms, which can take two to three hundred square feet of open space to do properly. Often the longer forms have so many movements that they require twenty minutes or more to complete. The thirteen-movement form is the perfect set for anyone wishing to practice Tai Chi within the time and space limitations of city life.

Wu Chi

According to Taoist cosmology, before the beginning of the manifested universe, there was a state of total emptiness. In this primordial state, nothing stirred. The relative concept of time did not apply to the primordial state, because there was nothing to measure time against. All was a void.

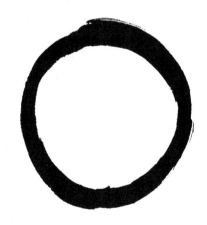

The empty circle symbolizes Wu Chi, the state of pure openness.

The ancient Taoists gave it a name. It was called Wu Chi. Wu means absence, negation, nothingness. The Chi in Wu Chi, even though it is spelled the same way in English as the word that means life force, is a totally different word in Chinese. The Chi in Wu Chi means "highest" or "ultimate." Wu Chi thus means "ultimate state of nothingness."

Tai Chi: The Primordial Yin and Yang

The Wu Chi stirred through some unknown impulse, and the first moment of creation began. This first impulse manifested as Chi through the primordial polarity of Yin and Yang, negative and positive. The interplay of Yin and Yang is the essential expression of Wu Chi. The Taoists named this process Tai Chi or "Supreme Ultimate." All the multiplicity of phenomena found in the universe, visible or invisible, are the result of Yin and Yang interaction.

The Tai Chi Diagram.

Chi: The Source of All Movement

Chi, or life force, is the foundation of all the Taoist practices, in the same way that electricity is the foundation of modern civilization. Without electricity, practically every aspect of our modern life style comes to a stop. Similarly, without Chi, one's life comes to an abrupt halt.

Chi can be defined as bio-electricity, life force, vitality, or simply energy. Chi is all of these, but none of them exclusively. Just as electricity is still incomprehensible to scientists in its total breadth and depth, Chi is beyond intellectual understanding.

According to the ancient Taoists, Chi is found in the air we breathe, yet it is not just oxygen or any of the other gaseous components of the atmosphere. Chi is also found in the food we eat, yet it is not just a vitamin, mineral, or carbohydrate that we can chemically isolate. Chi is absorbed into the food we eat through the process of photosynthesis, yet it is not sunlight or any other type of ray detectable by modern sensing devices.

Chi is the essence of the food we eat and the air we breathe, the real nourishment of the body. When we breathe or eat, we are taking Chi into our bodies. Without Chi, there can be no life.

THE FIVE ELEMENTS OR PHASES

The interaction of Yin and Yang is expressed through five basic phases of energy behavior, often called the Five Elements. The Five Elements refer not only to the five physical elements we find all around, but also to the five ways Chi expresses itself in the universe. The first phase is energy at rest, energy in an extreme state of quietness and concentration. This phase is named water, because water, if undisturbed, naturally becomes extremely still. The second phase is a development of the first; if energy is extremely quiet and concentrated, it bursts into activity at some point, just like the Wu Chi. This second phase is that expansion of energy. It is called wood, because trees burst into activity in the spring after their long period of winter rest. The burst of activity in the wood phase cannot last for long; it soon stabilizes into a period of sustained energy release. This third phase is named fire, because fire is able to sustain a high level of energy release over a long period. As the high energy-release rate of fire begins to decline, it gives rise to the fourth phase, that of contracting energy. The fourth phase is called metal, because metal is a very condensed state of energy. The fifth phase of energy is that of central balance and harmony of all the other four phases. This final phase is named earth, because the earth is the ground of all the other elements.

Yin/Yang is the root and trunk of all creation; the Five Elements are the branches that bear the leaves, flowers, and fruits of the universe. The result of the five phases of energy is the manifestation and activity of the sun, moon, stars, planets, and all life on earth.

This view of Taoist cosmology may seem abstract and simplistic, but modern science has arrived at essentially the same view of creation. All matter throughout the universe is made of atomic particles. The atoms, once believed to be the smallest indivisible particles of matter, have proved under observation to be made of subatomic particles and waves, all propelled into motion by the polarity of positive and negative. Scientists have also arrived at a concept of an original explosion of energy, which they refer to as the Big Bang.

Taoists view the universe as a vast ocean of interacting energy driven by the fundamental interplay of Yin and Yang. Humans are one of the most complex manifestations of such interaction.

The universe as a manifestation of the Five Elements is self-sustaining. All living creatures are constantly interacting with all the elements of creation through the processes of eating, breathing, sensing, feeling, and thinking.

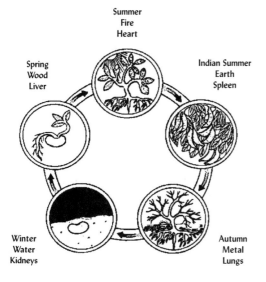

Summer
Fire
Heart

Spring
Wood
Liver

Indian Summer
Earth
Spleen

Winter
Water
Kidneys

Autumn
Metal
Lungs

The Five Elements

WHERE DO WE DERIVE OUR LIFE FORCE?

The basic source of human energy, according to Taoists, comes from our parents. The Yin energy of the mother in the egg and the Yang energy of the father in the sperm provide the initial sparks that ignite the fire of life. This energy from the parents is called prenatal energy or Original Chi.

A second source of Chi is radiation from the stars in the form of light, electromagnetic waves, and subsonic vibrations. The most prominent stars in this process are the sun, the North Star, and the stars in the constellation known as the Big Dipper.

Humans in particular depend on the Chi radiated through space by the stars and planets for sustenance. The air we breathe is charged with cosmic energy in the form of extremely fine particles of cosmic "dust." This dust is the residue of exploded stars, planets, and asteroids. It rains constantly onto the earth, forming an essential component of the soil.

Plants are the only living organisms that can directly transform light into nourishment. Humans absorb light energy indirectly by eating either vegetables or the flesh of other animals that feed on plants.

The interaction of light, cosmic dust in the soil, and air, together with water, forms the basis for photosynthesis in plants. All life on earth depends on plant life, either directly or indirectly. The great majority of organisms feed directly on plants, and a small minority feed on other animals that eat plants.

Through Taoist cultivation we accumulate abundant Chi in the lower Tan Tien. This Chi pressure can draw in more Chi life force from the universe around us.

Chi is life, and abundant energy is abundant life. If our energy supply is low due to illness or excessive emotions, we experience low vitality and lack of drive. Living ceases to be an enjoyable experience; we feel disconnected from the environment, from society, and from ourselves. Taoists therefore place extreme importance on cultivating and maintaining a high level of energy to strengthen one's connection with the universe and oneself.

The ultimate goal of Taoist practice is attaining a state of complete union with the source of the universe. All life emerges from Wu Chi unconsciously. Through Taoist practice one can attain immortality and return to the Wu Chi consciously to dissolve into oneness. Taoists actively encourage any practice or point of view that helps strengthen our connection with the universe.

The most direct way of sustaining our links with all creation is by cultivating the energy that is the foundation of all life. Tai Chi plays a central role in Taoism as one of the most efficient and effortless ways of cultivating Chi and experiencing one's own energetic origins. The precise Tai Chi postures open and undo energetic blockages in one's energy channels; the slow and gentle movements stretch one's energy channels and keep them strong and supple; the rhythmic movements of the muscles, spine, and joints pump energy through the whole body. Thus Tai Chi is an exercise that gives one more energy than it uses up, so after a round of Tai Chi one feels relaxed yet invigorated.

TAI CHI: A VITAL PART OF THE HEALING TAO SYSTEM

Although Tai Chi has been practiced by lay people for hundreds of years, it is within the overall context of Taoist practice that one can really understand Tai Chi's profound depth and importance. Historic and contemporary Taoist adepts practice Tai Chi as one part of their overall program for cultivating and developing their physical body, energy body, and spirit body. These three bodies correspond respectively to the Three Treasures or San Bao: Ching or Jing (sexual energy or essence), Chi (the inner breath, basic life force energy), and Shen (spirit or consciousness). All Taoist disciplines focus on strengthening these three aspects.

No one discipline can be said to cultivate all Three Treasures with equal emphasis and effectiveness. For this reason, most true practitioners use an integrated combination of practices to nourish the Three Treasures and thus to strengthen and develop the Three Bodies.

As we pointed out in the introduction, in the Healing Tao system we practice a combination of sitting, standing, and moving techniques that mutually support one another and create a strong foundation for mastering the internal arts.

THE MICROCOSMIC ORBIT

Many people have diligently practiced Tai Chi for several years, yet they do not have a clear idea of what Chi feels like. One of the requirements of advanced martial arts training is being able to sense the intention of the opponent before a move is made. If one is unable to sense one's own energy, it is impossible to sense the energy of anyone else, much less the Chi activating the opponent's thoughts before they manifest into action.

The first step in Tai Chi Chi Kung practice, therefore, is becoming acquainted with the force that animates one's being and learning to sense, direct, and circulate it through the Microcosmic Orbit.

The Microcosmic Orbit meditation is the foundation of all the Healing Tao practices. The Microcosmic Orbit is our main energetic circuit; it feeds all the other channels in the body. Opening the Orbit and removing blockages along its energetic pathway releases more Chi to vitalize the entire body. Through this practice, one learns to recognize what Chi feels like while circulating it through the Governor meridian (running up the back) and the Functional or Conception meridian (coming down the front of the body).

When one can feel Chi moving through the body, one can know whether one's Tai Chi posture is structurally correct by observing whether the posture opens or shuts off the energetic flow in the body. It is easier to learn the basics of Chi circulation during sitting meditation, when one is not distracted by having to move and pay attention to the hundreds of other details of the Tai Chi form. Once you have become familiar with the feeling of Chi circulation, you will easily begin to integrate this into your Tai Chi movements.

THE INNER SMILE AND THE SIX HEALING SOUNDS

The process of sensing one's own Chi is refined in Healing Tao practice through the Inner Smile and the Six Healing Sounds.

We communicate with our organs through the Inner Smile meditation, a process of connecting with the higher self and directing a loving and appreciative awareness to the various parts of the body. We have all experienced situations in which we are total strangers in new surroundings. Sometimes, if we are in a foreign country, we are not even able to speak the language, yet a smile automatically communicates to others that our intention is friendly. So smiling is a form of language, a friendly language, which we use in Taoist practice to communicate not only with other people but with our own vital organs and other parts of the body.

The Six Healing Sounds practice is a method for harmonizing and balancing the energy in the vital organs through movements, posture, and sound. Why communicate with the vital organs? In Taoist practice, we recognize that the vital organs are places in the body where Chi is absorbed, processed, stored, and made available for sustaining life. Becoming acquainted with the organs and sensing the Chi is essential for developing sensitivity to the needs of the body and the energy that gives it life. The Six Healing Sounds cool and detoxify the organs and help us release negative emotions that begin to restrict our energy flow.

At first the Inner Smile practice may seem disconnected from the Six Healing Sounds, but later we learn to smile down to the organ we are working with at the end of each sound.

Taoists believe consciousness is rooted not in the brain alone but also in the vital organs, and, in a more subtle and refined sense, in each of the cells. The Six Healing Sounds and the Inner Smile begin the process of listening to the body and developing deep inner sensitivity. By smiling to the organs and thanking them for the work they do, eventually we reawaken the intelligence of the whole body.

In the Healing Tao, therefore, we always begin Tai Chi Chi Kung practice with the Inner Smile. This helps the student relax and turn the awareness to the subtle inner sensations. Although the Six Healing Sounds are usually not directly integrated into a round of Tai Chi practice, performing them anytime during the day increases relaxation and inner awareness, and this enhanced state carries over to positively influence your Tai Chi.

Iron Shirt Chi Kung

In Healing Tao practice, energy work does not stop at sensing energy and establishing communication with the organs. Vital energy circulates within the entire structure of the physical body, so great care is taken to keep that structure in top shape.

We can have a high level of vitality, but if we constantly sit slumped, stand off center, or walk stooped forward, eventually we create a disfiguration of the skeletal structure. In addition, the organs are unnecessarily pressured and forced to perform under internal stress. The circulation of Chi then becomes blocked in places, causing energetic excesses and deficiencies that can eventually lead to illness.

To prevent or remedy damage to the physical and energetic structure, we teach a set of practices known as Iron Shirt Chi Kung. The word *Kung* in Chi Kung (or in Kung Fu) means *intensive work*. In Iron Shirt Chi Kung, we work intensively with three aspects of Chi: the Chi in the air we breathe, the prenatal Chi that has been in our bodies since conception, and the Chi in the organs.

We also work with the skeletal structure, the tendons, the connective tissue that surrounds all the organs and muscles, and the bone marrow. We learn to adjust the skeletal alignment in such a way that if a great force is applied to our structure, we can redirect it to the ground so that it does not throw us off balance. By learning how to place the skeletal structure in total alignment with the force of gravity, we

Tan Tien

If we know how to stand in alignment with the Heavenly and Earth Forces, then we can also learn to move with them.

also facilitate the movement of vital energy in the body.

The ancient Taoists firmly believed that any change in the physical body produces a similar change in the mind and emotions. Conversely, changes in the mental and spiritual being manifest through the physical body. The integration of the structure achieved through Iron Shirt practice is eventually reflected in a more balanced energy level, better health, and greater emotional and physical stability.

The intensive work done in Iron Shirt is relatively static; the different postures are all done standing rooted to one spot. But we are not like trees that never move! Putting the principles of Iron Shirt in motion, we arrive at the practice of Tai Chi.

HEALING LOVE THROUGH THE TAO

Ching Chi (or Jing Chi), the energy of our reproductive system, is the most condensed essence of energy in our bodies; just as a seed contains the entire tree, so too does our sexual energy contain the condensed essence of an entire human being.

In all life forms that multiply sexually, a tremendous amount of energy goes into the reproductive system. If this energy does not go into creating offspring and is not recycled into the body, it is simply lost. This loss is a great drain of life force; in fact, many plants die shortly after going to seed, and many animals die soon after reproducing.

Tai Chi Chi Kung practice helps lay the foundation for the Taoist inner alchemical transformation of Ching into Chi, Chi into Shen, and Shen into Wu Chi. Conservation of sexual energy is a prerequisite for transformation. It is therefore essential that the Tai Chi Chi Kung practitioner learn the methods of Healing Love Through the Tao for conserving sexual energy.

Healing Love also teaches one how to balance the Yin and Yang aspects of one's sexual energy. Many famous Tai Chi masters who did not know the Taoist secrets of love became too Yang, and sought to disperse their excess Yang in unhealthy ways such as sexual excess, drugs

and alcohol. Of course many of these masters died relatively young, failing to exemplify the fruits of long life that Tai Chi practice is famous for yielding.

BONE MARROW NEI KUNG

Tai Chi masters are also famous for having extraordinarily strong and dense bones, like steel wrapped in cotton. A recent experiment in China showed absolutely no evidence of osteoporosis in a group of both female and male Tai Chi practitioners over the age of eighty.

In Taoist physiology, the sexual essence is stored in the kidneys, the organs that rule the reproductive system. The kidneys also rule the bones, the marrow, and the brain. The Taoist sexual energy practices keep the reproductive organs fit and healthy. When Tai Chi is combined with the practices of Healing Love, Iron Shirt, and Bone Marrow Nei Kung, the essence of sexual energy is recycled and directed to the bones to strengthen and restore both the bone matrix and marrow.

INTEGRATING YOUR MEDITATIONS INTO MOVEMENT

Once the student has a clear sense of what Chi feels like, the next step is to learn to relax sufficiently to allow Chi and mind to move the structure. Once the student knows how to stand in alignment with the Heavenly and Earth forces, then it is not hard to learn to move in total alignment at all times. Once the student has developed a sense of rootedness to the ground, as well as mental focus and stability through meditation, then it is not hard to learn to carry these same qualities into daily activity.

The practice of Tai Chi is thus a further refinement of the sitting practice in Microcosmic Orbit meditation and the standing practices of Iron Shirt Chi Kung; it carries the centeredness developed in meditation and Iron Shirt into the movements of daily life, giving a more complete sense of well-being.

2
Why Practice Tai Chi Chi Kung?

The initial attraction of Tai Chi practice lies in the beauty and grace of its movements. Unlike the Japanese and Korean forms, Tai Chi does not require strenuous effort to accomplish. It can also be practiced into quite an advanced age without danger. By contrast, some of the "hard" forms of martial arts can cause severe damage to the joints if improperly practiced and are too vigorous for most elderly people.

TAI CHI CHI KUNG CAN IMPROVE POSTURE

One of the most important benefits of Tai Chi practice is the improvement it creates in posture. Poor posture results from a combination of negative emotional states and lack of self-awareness. We are all familiar with the picture of a chronically depressed person: stooped and weighed down at the shoulders, as if the whole world were pressing down on him or her. This posture reflects the negative emotional states of sadness, depression, indifference, withdrawal, arrogance, pride, fear, defensiveness, and so on. Once the negative emotions become chronically established, they are imprinted in the physical frame. These dysfunctional malformations then prevent the person from experiencing a harmonious and balanced emotional state.

Poor posture is a combination of negative emotional scars and lack of self-awareness.

One of the exercises we often do in workshops is to ask the participants first to sit in a fully energized position, allowing that posture to evoke the feelings of courage, grounding, strength, and emotional well-being. Then we ask the participants to slowly slump down in their chairs, heads hanging down. In this slumped position we allow them to experience the feelings of sadness, depression, and lack of energy.

When participants have experienced states of both high and low energy, we ask them to sit upright in a courageous, energizing posture and again try to experience sadness, depression, and lack of energy. After some time we ask them to slump down in their chairs and try to re-evoke the feelings of courage, grounding, strength, and harmony. The majority of people can neither recreate a harmonious state while slumped in the chair, nor feel depressed when sitting in the posture of proper alignment.

This simple experiment (which we encourage you to try) demonstrates the important relationship between posture and emotional states. If you are unconscious of how you stand and move, you usually remain unconscious of the subtle emotional states you are generating.

One reason meditation practice is an integral support of Tai Chi is that it generates a state of self-awareness. This self-awareness is twofold, encompassing awareness of both the energy moving within the meridians and of the structure within which the energy is moving.

The very first position of Tai Chi, Wu Chi Stance, initiates the process of postural awareness. Beginning at the soles of the feet, we sense to see if all the points of the feet are touching the ground. Moving upward, we sense whether one leg has more weight than the other, or if there is any subtle strain at the hips from leaning in any direction. At the shoulders, we sense whether there is tightness and observe if the scapulae are rounded so that the chest does not stick out. Reaching the head, we check the position of the chin and the base of the skull, making sure the chin is slightly tucked in, allowing for a feeling of openness at the base of the skull. Finally, we align the angle of the crown until we feel a subtle upward energy pull, focusing on a ball of Chi above our crowns. This pull indicates that the entire structure is fully suspended between the pull of the Heavenly force above and the Earth force below.

Structural alignment is a natural function of the human body, but we tend to lose it after childhood. Through Tai Chi practice, we consciously and constantly readjust the posture until proper structural alignment becomes part

Wu Chi Stance

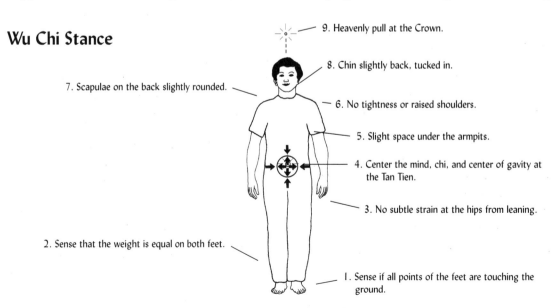

9. Heavenly pull at the Crown.

8. Chin slightly back, tucked in.

7. Scapulae on the back slightly rounded.

6. No tightness or raised shoulders.

5. Slight space under the armpits.

4. Center the mind, chi, and center of gavity at the Tan Tien.

3. No subtle strain at the hips from leaning.

2. Sense that the weight is equal on both feet.

1. Sense if all points of the feet are touching the ground.

of our natural bodily knowledge once again, and we no longer slump unconsciously for long. This improvement in physical posture is immediately reflected in improved mental and emotional structure. The self-awareness that awakens us to misaligned posture also awakens us to negative emotional states that we might not otherwise notice.

A slumped posture prevents the life force from moving efficiently.

Proper posture also plays a key role in healthy energy circulation. This was demonstrated in the previous exercise by sitting in the depressed and energized positions. One feels energized simply because the posture of courage allows the energy to flow better; similarly, one feels depressed because the slumped posture prevents the life force from moving efficiently.

Taoist practice has shown over thousands of years of experience that poor energy circulation plays a major role in illness. When we encourage proper energy circulation through meditation, exercise, and positive mental states, the incidence of illness decreases rapidly.

TAI CHI CHI KUNG STRENGTHENS THE NERVOUS SYSTEM

One of the most damaging aspects of contemporary life is the destructive effects of pollution, uncontrolled negative emotions, and urban overcrowding on the human central nervous system. The advertisements on television for remedies to relieve headache, stomach upset, insomnia, constipation, and so on reflect the sad state of the modern nervous system.

The nervous system is the electrochemical mechanism through which the body regulates all its functions. Life force, in the form of electromagnetic impulses, is the means the nervous system uses to effect communication. The improved energy circulation experienced through meditation and Tai Chi has a regenerating effect on the nervous system.

TAI CHI CHI KUNG CAN BENEFIT CHRONIC ILLNESSES

Another positive aspect of meditation and Tai Chi practice is their effect on illnesses already present. While reviewing many of the English publications on Tai Chi in preparation for this book, I was impressed by the life stories of the serious practitioners. Many of the great figures of contemporary Tai Chi began their Tai Chi practice due to serious illnesses that modern medicine had dismissed as chronic or terminal.

The improvement in energy circulation and the transformation of negative emotional and mental states are significant factors in the elimination of illnesses. Thanks to the work of modern researchers such as Dr. Bernie Siegel and Dr. Herbert Benson, Western medicine is beginning to recognize that certain chronic and terminal illnesses that do not respond to pharmaceutical or surgical treatments can be cured through a change in the mental and emotional outlook of the patient, combined with some form of energizing exercise.

TAI CHI CHI KUNG CAN CLEAR NEGATIVE EMOTIONS

Being able to move freely, calmly, and effortlessly is one of the natural traits of the healthy body. So is the ability to experience and express the complete range of human emotions, both positive and negative. Holding on to emotions and not releasing them fully is one of the main causes of tension and stress, creating blockages of energy flow and eventually leading to illness.

A clear and honest awareness of one's inner state is one of the results of successful meditation practice. This same awareness is expanded in Tai Chi practice, so that little by little one is able to notice in one's movement the subtle areas of tension and holding. Discovering an area of tightness and tension, one can become aware of the emotional pattern behind the "body armoring" that is causing the tension. One can then apply a wide range of methods to help dissolve it. Borrowing from the meditation practice of the Inner Smile, one can smile to these areas during Tai Chi practice and send positive feelings to dissolve tensions. One can also direct the life force to areas that need healing.

TAI CHI CHI KUNG BENEFITS THE CONNECTIVE TISSUE, TENDONS, MUSCLES, AND CIRCULATION OF CHI

The life force has a very definite physical structure through which it moves. Over the last thirty years, research has been carried out in Asia and the West to determine the precise pathways of the life force. Recent studies have focused on the role of the connective tissue in energy transmission.

The connective tissue, or fascia, is a very thin layer of tissue that pervades the whole organism, enveloping the organs, muscles, tissues, and bones. As its name implies, the connective tissue connects. The most visible aspect of the connective tissue is the fascia, but at the microscopic level, connective tissues extend into every cell in the body, linking each cell with the rest of the organism.

The most important research on the connective tissue (in terms of its relevance to Tai Chi) has focused on its bioelectrical and biochemical properties. It has been discovered that the connective tissue functions as a vast electrical communication system linking every single cell of the body with every other.

When viewed through a microscope, the connective tissue looks like a complex crystalline lattice structure. When we perform simple movements, the crystalline lattice structure is compressed, generating bioelectrical signals. It is now suspected that the traditional meridian system of Chinese medicine may be closely linked with the pervasive connective tissue.

In the vast repertoire of Taoist exercises, no practices can be found for developing bulky musculature, as in Western body building. The main reason is Taoist research on tendon

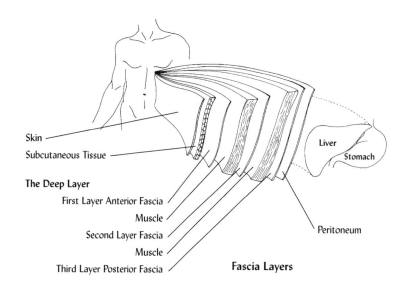

Skin
Subcutaneous Tissue

The Deep Layer
First Layer Anterior Fascia
Muscle
Second Layer Fascia
Muscle
Third Layer Posterior Fascia

Liver
Stomach

Peritoneum

Fascia Layers

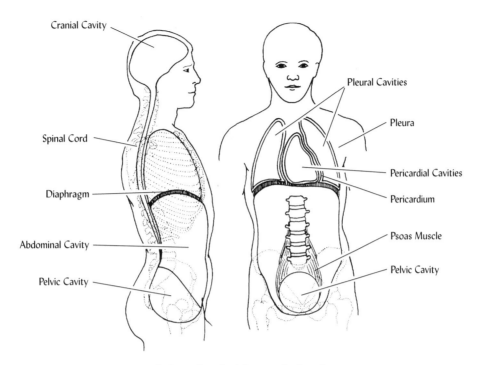

Cranial Cavity

Spinal Cord

Diaphragm

Abdominal Cavity

Pelvic Cavity

Pleural Cavities

Pleura

Pericardial Cavities

Pericardium

Psoas Muscle

Pelvic Cavity

Each organ has a fascia layer covering its cavity.

power. Muscles are developed through heavy physical exercise. Even if one trains everyday for the rest of one's life, there is an age at which the muscles begin to decline in strength and size. The muscle tissue breaks down and is no longer rebuilt as efficiently as in youth. Muscle tissue also demands many of the nutrients we take in to nourish and maintain itself.

The tendons, by contrast, are not affected by age and require very little vascularization for maintenance. If a person has developed strong tendons through a regimen of exercises, then that tendon power can be maintained until a ripe old age. The tendons act like thick rubber bands that naturally contract. Together with the muscles, the tendons facilitate the movement of the bone structure.

The practice of Iron Shirt Chi Kung introduces different methods for strengthening the tendons. One of the goals of Iron Shirt is to relax the muscles as much as possible, engaging the tendons to hold the structure while standing. This training carries over into Tai Chi practice.

The advantage of developing tendon power is that the musculature can then be more relaxed in movement. When there is muscular relaxation, the connective tissue is able to transport electrical impulses and life force much more efficiently. In Tai Chi one learns how to move in a state of muscular relaxation, allowing the tendons and the life force in the connective tissue to provide the "inner" strength.

1. The connective tissue has a lattice structure.
2. When exercise is performed, the lattice structure compresses, generating bioelectrical signals.

3

Basic Principles of Tai Chi Chi Kung

Tai Chi Chi Kung is grounded in the principles of the Tao. The extent to which you have incorporated and integrated these principles into your movements determines your level of mastery. It does not matter if you know a long or a short Tai Chi form; what counts is knowledge and application of the Tai Chi principles.

This chapter introduces the basic principles of Tai Chi Chi Kung. Study them, memorize them, and apply them in your movements. The best way to practice at first is to take one principle at a time and work on it until you can do it automatically, without conscious thought. Then work on the next principles in the same way until you have mastered them all.

The second half of this book introduces the more advanced Tai Chi Chi Kung principles. Do not worry about learning these until you have mastered the more basic principles included in this chapter and have gained competence in the Tai Chi Chi Kung form (or another Tai Chi style) as presented in Chapter 5.

Eventually, with daily practice you will discover that you have incorporated the Tai Chi principles into your daily life; as you sit, walk, stand, and lie down, you will notice that you are moving in a fresh, effortless, and beautiful way. This is the reward of Tai Chi Chi Kung.

STAY ROOTED IN EACH MOVEMENT

Rooting means being connected with the ground. All forms of energy work require that one remain solidly rooted. Unfortunately, rooting is poorly understood outside martial arts circles. Many long-time practitioners of meditation have never even heard of rooting. Imag-

All forms of energy work require that
we remain solidly connected to the ground.

In Tai Chi, rooting means more than just standing on the ground. Rooting begins with the mental, emotional, and spiritual aspects of the personality.

ine an electrician who has never heard about grounding the equipment! He is bound for disaster sooner or later.

Tai Chi practice integrates physical rooting into the very way one moves through life. The practice of psychic rooting is cultivated through meditation. Physical and energetic rooting is developed through Iron Shirt and Tai Chi, as a support to the mental and emotional changes that take place via meditation. One reflects the other. The grounding cultivated through Tai Chi manifests as stability in movements. Emotionally, it manifests as a stable personality with clarity of purpose and full command of the willpower. As an aspect of spiritual cultivation in the Tao, rooting is very important; Tai Chi and Iron Shirt practice develop this ability.

Tai Chi is also a martial art, and its emphasis on rooting is one of the facets that has made Tai Chi a superior system of self-defense. In Tai Chi, power and stability come from structural alignment with the ground. A person becomes very hard to knock over when aligned; the opponent may feel as if he or she has just run into a solid tree with deep roots. When one attacks, it is with the support of the earth behind one's movements. This aligned force is then directed, with all the parts of the skeletal framework working together with integrity.

By contrast, many martial artists train specific parts of the body in isolation. They work to develop strong arm and leg muscles in particular, and when they punch, they are mainly using the strength of the arm and shoulder.

How can one part of the body acting alone be as powerful as the united and integrated strength of the whole body? Other martial art styles may use the force of the waist and legs in punches, but if the practitioners are not rooted and do not have correct structural alignment, they still lack true power.

MAINTAIN YOUR CENTER OF GRAVITY IN THE LOWER TAN TIEN

In Tai Chi one seeks to maintain perfect balance and stability throughout all one's movements, both in solo practice of the Tai Chi form and in Tai Chi martial arts applications. For optimum stability, in Tai Chi one trains to keep the center of gravity low in the body, in the area between the navel, the Door of Life, and the sexual center—the approximate midpoint of the body. This area is known as the lower Tan Tien. Keeping the center of gravity in the lower Tan Tien is relatively easy as long as one is sitting. The moment one stands up and begins to move, the center of gravity adjusts itself to the particular movement one is doing.

A baby's first attempt at moving around in the world is crawling. A baby crawling on the floor has a low center of gravity. Later, as its leg bones began to solidify, the baby attempts to stand up. For a few weeks the baby goes through the process of standing and falling until it learns the trick of raising its center of gravity and staying centered. From there, the child gradually accomplishes the more difficult feats of walking, trotting, running, bicycle riding, and sports, where balance is refined to a higher degree.

Ordinarily we keep the center of gravity floating between the chest and the lower abdomen.

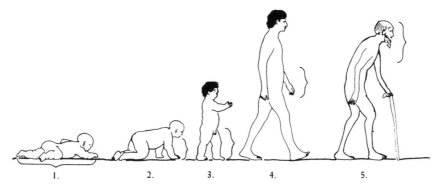

1. The center of gravity is very low. 2. Center of gravity slightly higher. 3. Center balanced between navel and legs.
4. Center balanced between abdomen and solar plexus. 5. Center very high, between upper head and chest.

As one grows older, one's center of gravity rises to a fluctuating point in the torso. As one experiences negative emotions, the center of gravity begins to travel farther upward into the torso. When a person becomes angry, the center of gravity can rise up to the chest, causing enough energetic pressure to produce a heart attack. In extreme fright, the center of gravity may rise all the way to the throat, making the person unable to utter a sound.

Excessive anger can bring the center of
gravity high up in the chest or the throat.

By the time a person reaches adulthood, the center of gravity may be permanently based somewhere in the upper chest, making the person top heavy. Thus elderly people tend to fall easily and often need the assistance of walking sticks.

The process of relearning to become centered is easier at first while sitting or standing in one place than it is in movement. In the Healing Tao system, therefore, the Microcosmic Orbit meditation and Iron Shirt practices are taught before Tai Chi.

In the Microcosmic Orbit meditation, the practitioner begins by learning to focus the awareness at the Tan Tien area, the midpoint of the body. As the breath becomes even and the body relaxes, the center of gravity naturally drops down to the navel area. In Iron Shirt, a similar process takes place. The person stands in any of five positions, and by exhaling, relaxing the chest and diaphragm, and controlling the breath at the lower abdomen, the center of gravity shifts down to the lower Tan Tien.

The next stage in working with the center of gravity is to move the structure while keeping the center low at all times. This sounds simple, but it takes practice. In Tai Chi, one keeps the center of gravity low by learning to move in alignment with the Heavenly and Earth forces, generating the movements from the hips, and remaining mentally and physically connected to the ground.

Centeredness and grounding are brought about not only by mechanical knowledge of the physical structure but also by corresponding emotional and mental states. If one is able to experience emotions and then let go and relax, the center of gravity returns to a place somewhere in the lower torso and all is well. However, if one never lets go of emotions and tends to dwell in the past, one will lack presence. One's body will be characterized by a high center of gravity.

Through meditation practice, one learns to keep the mind centered at the Tan Tien. The Tan Tien energy, guided by the mind, directs all movements. In Tai Chi this practice is developed further; Tai Chi practice uses the mental power developed through meditation to direct the life force to any bodily point. If one wishes to turn left, for example, the mind directs the Tan Tien Chi to turn left, and the energy guides the hips into the turn. The same applies to moving forward or sinking back.

A person with a high center of gravity lives disconnected from the ground.

KEEP THE BODY VERTICALLY ALIGNED AS IF SUSPENDED FROM THE CROWN

Another Tai Chi principle is to keep your body aligned with gravity, awakening the thrusting channels that penetrate through the body's core as a central axle around which you can pivot freely and easily. This is also described as feeling the head as if it is suspended from a string attached to a Chi ball or star above your head. In a misdirected effort to keep the spine erect, many people struggle to stretch the head up from below. Instead, train yourself to guide the Chi flow into the spine. This stretches and lifts the spine effortlessly

The effortlessness of Chi erecting the spine.

upward. Awareness of Chi at the crown (the Bai Hui point, Governing Vessel 20) calms and relaxes you while aligning your body with the Heavenly force.

Gravity acts on the physical structure by exerting a vertical pull in relation to the ground. This vertical pull aligns from the crown through the perineum to the soles of the feet. In Tai Chi movements, one maintains this central line of gravity, whether one is moving forward, sinking back, or turning. All movements emanate from the center, both physically and mentally.

Subtle pull on the crown

Eyes looking ahead
Chin slightly back
Shoulders equal height
Chest slightly sunk in

Lower Tan Tien Chi pressure

Hands equal height

Equal weight on both legs – no leaning sideways

Equal weight both feet – all nine points touching the ground

If on stands fully erect, feeling suspended from a string, the energy flows up, energizing the organs and generating a feeling of well-being.

If a person stands straight, with the central line of gravity running from the crown through the perineum and down to the feet perfectly aligned, the weight is equally distributed over the nine points of the feet. This is called perfect balance of the Heaven and Earth forces.

When one leans one way or another, the central line of gravity no longer runs from the crown down through the perineum. The line of gravity changes according to whichever way one is leaning, and it is no longer equally distributed over the nine points of the feet.

For example, when the body leans just a little forward, there is more weight on the ball of the foot and less on the heel. The center of gravity, according to one's height, weight, and flexibility, is high up somewhere in the chest. If a per-

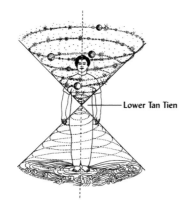

Perfect balance harmonizes and balances Heavenly and Earth forces at the Tan Tien.

son is shoved or pulled while in this position, he or she will fall forward easily.

Many people have the habit of leaning forward when walking. When one walks leaning forward with a high center of gravity, one is actually falling; what prevents one from falling down totally is the rapid movement of the legs. One automatically experiences excess tension as a result, which drains the energy. Through habit, one may become numb to what is actually happening, but the nervous system knows better, and one experiences deep tiredness and fatigue because of this uneconomical use of energy.

Leaning forward changes the path of the central line of gravity.

The habit of leaning has a destructive effect on both the physical body and the energy circulation. Leaning causes compression in certain organs, affecting their energy flow. Leaning also disturbs the pumping action of the diaphragm, so the heart has to work harder to

pump the blood. Any interference with the diaphragm affects the breath and ultimately the mind. Energy blockages created through leaning eventually distort the physical structure, the powers of the mind, and the emotions.

Hip and spinal cord problems often result from not having the weight evenly distributed over the nine points of the feet. One can observe from the way the soles of one's shoes wear out how evenly one stands and walks on the feet.

Note that there are certain Tai Chi styles, notably Wu style, in which the practitioners may appear to lean forward when pushing. Yet if we analyze their structure, we find that the spine remains straight and perpendicular to the hip bone, exactly as if they were standing straight. What appears to be a high center of gravity is counterbalanced by the extension of the rear leg, so the center of gravity remains in the lower Tan Tien. It is like a stick, leaning at an angle yet firmly connected to the ground. The "leaning" stance in these Tai Chi styles is just as effective as the vertical stances used in the Tai Chi Chi Kung form.

BREATHE WITH THE LOWER ABDOMEN

When a baby emerges from the womb, the first thing it does is take a deep breath. We can survive without food for weeks, we can live without water for several days, but we cannot do without oxygen for more than a few minutes.

Breathing is both a voluntary and an involuntary function of the body. We can consciously change the way we breathe and even stop breathing at will, but we cannot voluntarily hold the breath to the point of suffocation; there is an automatic mechanism in the body which prevents us from doing that. In accident cases in which the victim has stopped breathing, the most immediate danger to the organism is brain damage. So breathing and brain function are intimately connected.

Ancient Taoists discovered that the breath is connected not only with the brain but with consciousness itself. Taoist meditators of the past left a tremendous written legacy in the collection of more than a thousand volumes collectively known as the Taoist Canon. Many of these texts focus on the importance of breathing and present numerous breathing methods for health and spiritual development. This extensive repertoire of breathing exercises makes Taoism one of the world's most comprehensive yogas.

If the breath is calm, even, and steady, the mind experiences these same qualities. Conversely, if the breath is labored, rough, or uneven, the mind is affected by all sorts of wavering feelings and emotions. The next time you see someone get very angry, notice his or her breathing pattern. Numerous modern therapies recommend deep, even, rhythmic breathing exercises as a means of restoring calmness to emotionally disturbed patients.

Tai Chi practice is always done in conjunction with abdominal breathing. Abdominal breathing is sometimes misunderstood to involve breathing air into the lower abdomen, but in fact air can only be breathed into the lungs.

Abdominal breathing simply means keeping the abdomen relaxed while breathing. During inhalation, the diaphragm moves down, and during exhalation it moves up. If the lower abdominal muscles are relaxed during inhalation, the abdomen can expand, there is more room for the diaphragm to move down, and more air is taken into the lungs. We breathe more fully and are therefore more energized.

If the abdomen is constricted by muscular tension, the diaphragm cannot expand fully. We automatically compensate by expanding the chest; this is called shallow chest breathing. Chest breathing is less energizing because the lungs cannot expand as much as during abdominal breathing. Physiologically, the intercostal muscles of the chest are designed to provide only about 25 percent of the muscular force necessary to fill the lungs. The remaining 75 percent of effort is the diaphragm's job.

Lower abdominal breathing helps keep the center of gravity low. It is associated with calmness and relaxation. High chest breathing and keeping a high center of gravity are neurologically associated with stress, anxiety, and hypertension. One recent research study revealed that over 70 percent of hypertensive patients were high chest breathers. In another British study, over 90 percent of agoraphobic patients (people with an irrational fear of leaving the house) were successfully treated simply by teaching them to shift the breath into the lower abdomen when phobic symptoms began to occur. The next time you see someone get upset, observe whether he or she is breathing with the lower abdomen, or whether the chest is heaving up and down. Emotional balance is easily restored by the calming effect abdominal breathing has on the mind.

Lower abdominal breathing also benefits the circulation of blood. The heart is the main organ responsible for pumping blood throughout the body. When the diaphragm moves up and down freely in respiration, this movement increases and decreases the pressure in the lower abdominal cavity, through which the aorta and vena cava flow. This creates a pumping action that effectively reduces the heart's workload by assisting the venous blood to return to the heart. The lower abdomen thus serves as a second heart.

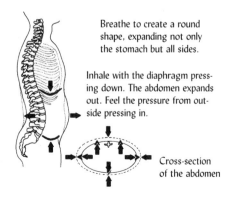

Breathe to create a round shape, expanding not only the stomach but all sides.

Inhale with the diaphragm pressing down. The abdomen expands out. Feel the pressure from outside pressing in.

Cross-section of the abdomen

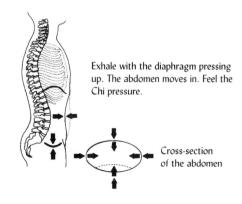

Exhale with the diaphragm pressing up. The abdomen moves in. Feel the Chi pressure.

Cross-section of the abdomen

Lower abdominal breathing helps keep
the center of gravity in the lower Tan Tien.

In bottle breathing, the lowest part of the bottle fills up first.

Constipation caused by abdominal tension can often be relieved by the gentle massaging action of abdominal breathing as well.

Abdominal breathing is easier when the body relearns to keep the spine aligned with the Earth and Heavenly forces. If the spine is always bent forward, the diaphragm cannot move freely during respiration.

Lower abdominal breathing is the natural way to breathe; every healthy baby is born knowing how to do it. As we get older and experience the stresses and traumas of life, we become hardened physically, emotionally, and mentally. Little by little, the muscles of the abdomen and the diaphragm become tight in some places and flabby in others, and we lose most of our inherent ability to breathe deeply.

Relearning abdominal breathing requires two things: first, one must loosen up emotionally; and second, one must strengthen the abdominal muscles that have become weak from lack of use.

The most effective way of cultivating even breath is through the practice known as bottle breathing. Bottle breathing is named for the way liquid fills an empty bottle. When liquid is poured into a bottle, the liquid fills the bottle from the bottom up.

Deep breathing is exactly the same. The nose is the opening, and the lower abdomen is the bottom of the bottle. In bottle breathing, one learns to inhale gently and steadily, relaxing the muscles of the lower abdomen. As the air penetrates and expands the lungs, there is an expansion of the diaphragm downward. If the muscles of the abdomen are relaxed, then the diaphragm's downward expansion makes the lower abdomen expand.

To learn abdominal breathing, there is a very simple exercise that can be done in bed just before sleeping. Simply lie down on the back, legs and arms extended and relaxed. The clothes should be wide and loose, especially at the waist. Place a heavy book or brick on the lower abdomen. Inhale slowly and as deeply as possible, then exhale slowly and steadily through the parted lips until all the air is exhaled. Close the mouth and begin to inhale through the nose slowly but steadily, watching the book rise as the abdomen expands. You may place the head on a pillow to more easily see the book rise and fall with the breath.

Learn to build up the Chi pressure.

This simple exercise of abdominal weight-lifting allows the body to become reacquainted with the lower abdominal muscles. Over a period of regular practice, this greatly strengthens the abdomen.

During Iron Shirt Chi Kung practice, we regularly combine lower abdominal breathing with "packing breath", inhaling into the lower abdomen while pulling up on the anal muscles and gently pressing down with the diaphragm.

In Tai Chi, it is not necessary to practice the packing breath per se, but we still combine lower abdominal breathing with a subtle tightening of the anal muscles. We call this "sealing the bottom", and it prevents the energy from leaking out through flaccid anal muscles.

Maintaining a firm but gentle Chi pressure in the lower abdomen is the heart of developing the Chi for Tai Chi practice. When you inhale, feel the lower abdomen inflating and expanding to form a Chi pressure ball in the Tan Tien; simultaneously feel a corresponding pressure pushing in from outside. As you exhale, lightly press the Chi ball down with your diaphragm and abdominal muscles. You should feel the inside pressure pressing out and at the same time feel the outer pressure pressing in.

Gradually you will feel an internal Chi ball building up inside. Once you do, you can start to spiral the Chi ball and slowly move the Chi ball down to the coccyx and up the spine, up to the crown of the head, down to the tongue and down the front of your body to the navel, and back to the Tan Tien. Soon you can guide the Chi to the arms and legs.

Because the series of Tai Chi movements is performed slowly, it is possible to learn to regulate the breath and calm the mind. The regulation of breath begins by learning how to breathe with the abdomen, but eventually, as the body opens up and the energy begins flowing, a Tai Chi practitioner feels as if he or she is breathing with the whole body.

Meditation practice is one of the best methods for learning to regulate the breath. Once one has learned to regulate the breath through sitting or standing meditation, one learns to sustain regulated breath in movement through Tai Chi practice; hence, Tai Chi is often called moving meditation. The proper structure within each movement allows the breath to permeate the whole organism.

Breathing low down into the abdominal region, breathing through the skin, and breathing into the bone marrow are learned in Iron Shirt Chi Kung. In Tai Chi we combine these breathing techniques with relaxation and energy circulation and then put it all into motion.

OPEN THE JOINTS THROUGH GENTLE INWARD ROTATION

Another important part of Tai Chi is opening all the joints in the body. The stresses of modern life often first affect the joints (arthritis) and particularly the spinal vertebrae (back problems). Stress on the spinal cord obstructs the flow of Chi. These obstructions further affect the organs, glands, and immune system, eventually leading to illness.

Taoists regard the joints as energy gates or centers where the Chi can be stored and generated. The tendons are linked to these centers. All the Tai Chi movements develop these centers by opening the joints and strengthening the tendons so the Chi and tendon force can be stored and released at will.

With Tai Chi practice, the Taoists found, small internal movements generate joint-stored Chi and its associated tendon force, while the big external movements generate muscle force. Through the way of internal development, when the joints are filled to capacity with Chi, the Chi begins to fill the bones. The inner rotation of the joints and tendons must be performed slowly, using the mind to guide the Chi to the joints and tendons, the joint will open and act like a cushion. Then the Chi can be absorbed into the bones. With fast movement, there is no time for the mind to guide and direct the Chi absorption. This parallels the way of nature. The strongest of the trees are not the ones that shoot up quickly; the strongest trees grow slowly over hundreds of years.

The hip joint is the first joint we train to open. This joint is part of the kua, which also includes the psoas muscles and the soft tissue, vessels and meridians of the inguinal region. When the hip joint is closed, the groin becomes blocked and the blood vessels, lymph and nerves in the inguinal area will fold and close. This causes circulation problems and the Chi will not flow freely. To practice opening the groin and hip joint, keep the knees loose and open, but not bent too much. Learn to sink down from the hip joint first, and feel the weight drop directly from the pelvis to the heels, not to the knees. To further help the hip joints open, concentrate on the ankle joints and direct the Chi from the hip joint into the ankle joint and then into the big toes.

The spinal joints are the second joints that we focus on opening. To open the spinal joints, you can practice building the Chi in the lower Tan Tien (abdomen), feeling the Chi ball and the Chi pressure there. Use the mind to spiral the Chi in the abdomen, like a ball rolling from front to back, and let the energy build up. Then guide the Chi into the coccyx and up the spine, pushing the energy into the spaces between the discs which separate the vertebrae. This will elongate the spine. You can also use meditation to help feel the Chi open the spine. Feel a string through the center of the spine pulling the crown of the head upward. Imagine the string is connected with a star overhead; feel this string lift the body and elongate the spine. Once the spine opens, the energy will flow to T-2 and C-7 and down to the arms and hands.

To help open all of the joints in the body, grow the Chi in the joints of the index fingers and the big toes.

INTEGRATE THE ENTIRE STRUCTURE AND SPIRAL THE EARTH FORCE

The Earth force begins to travel up the legs when we are able to do three things together. First, we relax the feet to connect with the Earth force. Second, we spiral the foot outward to create a screwing motion upward. Third, we push upward as if we were going to jump.

These three actions in rapid succession allow the Earth force to travel upward.

Once the Earth force spirals up to the hip, we allow it to continue up the spine by turning the hips to fully face the object of discharge. This hip motion allows the rising Earth force to continue spiraling up the spine to the C-7 vertebra, the juncture of the arms and neck.

We then allow the Earth force to continue spiraling out of the discharging arm by sinking the chest and moving the chin slightly back, as if recoiling from a push. This combination of movements takes place in an instant. All these seemingly separate actions of spiraling and discharge work only if all the movements are actually coordinated as one motion, so we must become quite skillful at moving in one piece.

Hips turn

Ankles and knees spiral

Press feet to the ground

Spiraling Part 2: Turn the hip to face fully forward and let the force spiral to T-11.

Push and Spiral the arms inward as if turning a screwdriver.

Spiraling Part 3: Sink chest, chin back.

Spiraling Part 1:1. Press feet down and spiral leg outward.
2. Press down and push upward as if to jump and the Chi will help push open the joints.

The ability to spiral the Earth force properly is not a purely mechanical skill. As in all aspects of Tai Chi, the mind plays a central role. Without the ability to focus the mind in one single point, the force one is trying to discharge becomes dissipated in varying degrees. The practitioner should integrate the mind, body, and spirit into one. Opening the Belt Channels through the Fusion of the Five Elements meditation greatly enhances one's ability to spiral the Chi around and through the body.

DISTRIBUTE THE WEIGHT OVER THE NINE POINTS OF THE FEET

The human structure is like a tree. The roots are in the feet, the torso and legs are the trunk, and the arms are the branches. The inner foundation of Tai Chi is the life force; the outer foundation is the feet. The feet support the whole body's weight, and at the same time they connect with the Earth force. In Taoism the feet are considered the ground wire of the body.

A chair or table is most stable when its weight is equally supported by all four legs. Similarly, we are most stable when the weight is evenly divided over the nine points of the foot. These nine points are the heel, outer edge, small ball, large ball, and five toes. In Tai Chi, we take great care to place these nine points evenly in contact with the ground each time we step and shift weight. Then the weight is poised over the middle of the foot, a point known as the Bubbling Spring. This point is so named because when we align the balance over this point, the Earth energy seems to freely flow up into the body just like a bubbling geyser.

K-1:
The Bubbling Spring Point

K-1 and the Nine Points of the foot

GENTLY TWIST THE ANKLE JOINTS

The ankle joints are where one begins the process of transferring the body force and Chi to and from the ground to the torso and arms. When one can properly press the soles of the feet and gently twist the ankle joints, this helps transfer the weight into the ground. Similar to the way a propeller converts fluid force into motion, this rotation converts body force to Earth force, which can then travel up the leg to the spine, adding to one's internal structural strength.

Twisting the ankle joint very slightly outward while pressing the foot to the earth helps transfer the Earth force up.

GENTLY SPIRAL THE KNEE JOINTS

The spiraling action that begins with the ankle joints now connects to the knee joint, the next vital element in transferring the Earth force from the ground to the hip. This is done by placing the feet firmly on the ground and lightly twisting the femur bone with a slight twist at the knees. This action twists and crosses the tibia and fibula of the calves, creating an extremely strong force. Tests have shown that when one twists in this way, the bones can withstand up to 2,000 pounds (one ton) of force.

When this knee twisting is performed properly, all the tendons are rotationally wrapped around the bone, creating a strong spring force. In this position, the Earth, knee, and hip are in one line of power. Instead of the knee supporting the full weight of the body, the weight is transferred to the ankles and then to the heels and soles through to the ground. In

When the knee is twisted out, all the tendons wrap around the bone, directing the energy flow upward.

Open the groin and lengthen the Psoas.

To transfer Earth force from the ground up, twist the knee joint slightly out.

this same way, the rebounding force that springs up from the Earth passes through the knees and does not jam there.

With all this twisting, it is important to reemphasize the lightness and gentleness of the desired motion. The knee is a delicate joint, and you should not overtwist it. Listen to your

When the knees are spiraled out, the force goes to the back of the leg and spirals down to the foot and the earth.

body; if you feel joint pain, stop! To perform Tai Chi properly, you must not use great force, but rather you should slowly grow the force inwardly. Eventually you will mainly use mind/eye/heart power, and all the forces will move in combination spontaneously.

If the knee is overtwisted, the force puts a great deal of stress on the knee joint.

Gastrocnemius Muscle

Soleus Muscle

Peroneus Longus and Tendon

Extensor Digitorum Longus Muscle

Tibialis Anterior

Muscles on the outside and back of the leg are activated through the feet pressing firmly against the ground and the knee spiraling outwards.

OPEN THE KUA AND ALIGN THE HIPS AND SACRUM

The positions of the hip joint and sacrum are very important in Tai Chi. One begins by opening the groin, or kai kua in Chinese, which translates loosely as "extending the base to become firmer and stronger." The name implies the importance placed on the stretch in this area. The significance of the groin in producing power through all the pushing motions of Tai Chi cannot be overemphasized. When the two knees are gently twisted as described above, the hip joints are opened outward, and the tendons in the groin area become firm. This allows the transfer of force from the legs into the trunk.

The sacral alignment determines whether your structure is strong or weak. By relaxing the lower back and slightly dropping the pelvis and sacrum as if you were tucking the tailbone between the legs, you structurally align the sacrum to the spine. When you feel the feet press more firmly into the ground, you have also aligned the sacrum to the legs, and you feel a line of power from the feet, to the groin, to the sacrum, and up the spine.

When you tuck the sacrum and press the feet into the ground, the spine becomes totally aligned.

The sacrum is also one of the major pumps for cerebrospinal fluid, which cushions the many nerves housed within the spine. The sacrum also helps pump the Chi up the spine. Activating the sacrum by tilting and releasing it thus enhances the activities of the central nervous system.

Successfully opening the kua depends in no small way upon the relaxing of the psoas muscles. Tai Chi Chi Kung, Iron Shirt Chi Kung and Tao Yin are internal exercise systems that attempt to lengthen and free up the function-

ing of these muscles. Awareness of the psoas muscles in Tai Chi Chi Kung is vitally important. The mechanical power of Tai Chi comes from using the integrated strength of the whole body. Because the psoas muscles connect from the lower vertebrae to the lower kua (or inguinal and hip joint region), they are a major key in linking the power of the legs to the spinal column.

The psoas muscles are also closely connected to the latissimus dorsi muscles, which extend from the upper spine to the humerus and shoulder bones. Therefore the psoas muscles are an important bridge between the lower and upper body. If the psoas muscles are relaxed and supple, the power of the legs can flow unimpeded, like a wave from the legs to the spine and then out through the arms.

ACTIVATE THE CHI BELT AT THE WAIST

The Tan Tien, also known as the Ocean of Chi, is in the lower abdominal area, which stores and activates the Original Chi. When it is developed, the Chi expands out to the kidneys, liver, spleen, small and large intestines, and sexual center. This internal expansion expresses itself outwardly, forming a Chi belt like a sash around the waist.

The Chi belt acts as a major bridge linking the lower part of the trunk to the upper part. If the Chi belt is not developed properly, the feet, legs, and hips have no connection to the upper body. They are like soldiers without a general: no control and ultimately no power.

When activating the Chi belt, feel equal pressure from both inside and out.

The word Chi in the context of the Chi belt refers to the combination of breath and energy. Through Iron Shirt Chi Kung, one learns to use the diaphragm to increase the lower abdominal pressure all the way around the waist. The increased pressure is similar to the role of air in a tire or mortar between bricks. The pressure helps fill in any weak spaces in one's structure and ties the upper and lower body together. But the force is not static and unconscious; it is dynamic, lively, and aware, able to move with the changing movements of Tai Chi. This dynamic quality is the energy component of the Chi belt.

The psoas muscles are next to the kidneys and the Door of Life point. The Door of Life is the back door to the Tan Tien, where our Original Chi is stored. When the psoas muscles are relaxed, the Original Chi can easily flow out into the channels and energize our movements. Furthermore, the Taoist Canon states that the connection between the kidneys (Water element) and the heart (Fire element) is the foundation of Yin and Yang balance in the body. The kidneys are like the root, the spine is like the stem, and the heart is like the flower. The water aspect of the kidneys cools the heart, while the fire aspect of the heart warms the kidneys. When the psoas muscles are loose and supple, the energy flows freely between the kidneys, spine, and heart.

The psoas muscles are also closely connected to the diaphragm. If the psoas muscles are supple, you can breathe more deeply and easily

and can fully use the power of the diaphragm and breath to support one's movements and help link the lower and upper body together through the Chi Belt.

DIRECT YOUR FORCE THROUGH THE SPINAL COLUMN: THE POWER TRAIN

Mistake: Excessive arching of the back.

The spinal column is formed from twenty-four vertebral bones plus the sacrum and coccyx. It connects the head, arms, and legs. For the Chi to pass back and forth between the head and limbs, it must go through the spinal column. Alignment of the spine is thus an essential part of Tai Chi practice.

Spinal misalignment, constricted abdomen, and negative emotions prevent the diaphragm from moving freely.

The spine, when properly aligned, is full of power and can greatly amplify the force from the legs to the arms or from the arms to the feet. By slightly tilting the sacrum and rounding the T-11, T-5, and C-7 vertebrae, one draws the spine like a bow about to shoot an arrow.

Correct: When the spine is aligned with gravity and just slightly bent outward, you will feel all the joints open.

SINK THE CHEST, SHOULDERS, AND ROUND THE SCAPULAE

The arms are connected to the trunk via the clavicle in the front and the scapulae in the back. Several groups of muscles, tendons, ligaments, and connective tissues keep the bones in place and allow free movement. The point of contact between the arm and the shoulder is at the joint of the scapula and the humerus bone.

The scapulae connect with the back in a structurally aligned way when you stretch the scapulae forward and at the same time sink the shoulder and sternum. In Iron Shirt Chi Kung practice, there is a position called Embracing the Tree that is particularly useful in learning to round the scapulae and sink the shoulder and chest.

Sinking the chest is done by exhaling a little, relaxing the chest muscles, and allowing the sternum to sink. As the sternum sinks, there is a corresponding movement of the scapulae laterally and forward.

Sinking the sternum also activates the thymus gland (located behind the

Sink the shoulders

upper sternum), an endocrine gland important to the immune system. The whole process takes place automatically when one hugs a big tree or big ball. If one is a chronic shallow chest breather with lots of accumulated tension in the chest muscles, there is very little flexibility in the sternum. If one attempts to sink the chest in such a situation, the shoulders usually go up as a compensating factor.

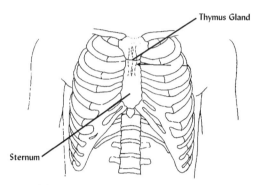

Thymus Gland

Sternum

Sinking the sternum helps activate the thymus gland.

Training in Iron Shirt Chi Kung is a great help in learning to relax the chest and diaphragm. The packing breath (taught in Iron Shirt Chi Kung), applied along the different points of the abdomen and up the spine, releases long-accumulated tensions and strengthens the muscles, tendons, tissues, and bone marrow.

In addition, the Embracing the Tree position is a perfect blueprint for the Thirteen Movement Tai Chi form. As we shall see in Chapter 4, familiarity with Iron Shirt facilitates Tai Chi. That is why, in the Healing Tao, Tai Chi is considered "Iron Shirt in motion."

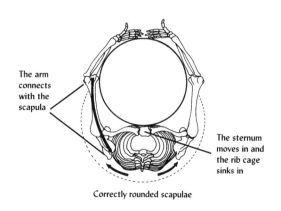

The arm connects with the scapula

The sternum moves in and the rib cage sinks in

Correctly rounded scapulae

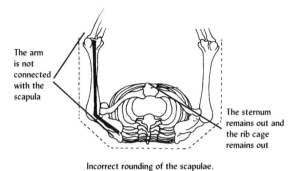

The arm is not connected with the scapula

The sternum remains out and the rib cage remains out

Incorrect rounding of the scapulae.

All the tendons, muscles, and ligaments are fully extended from the spine across the back, through the shoulders and arms, to the fingertips.

Rounding the scapulae and sinking the chest are key factors in energy discharge, but they are not the only elements. The position of the feet and knees is what allows the Earth energy to begin moving up the legs and into the spine, providing a gentle healing energy to the entire body.

Rounding the Scapulae

ACTIVATE AND ALIGN THE ER CHUI HSIA POINT (T-2) AND THE TA CHUI POINT (C-7) AND T2

The T-2 point is located just below the spinous process of T-2. The 7th cervical vertebrae (C-7) is the big spinal process at the base of the neck. The Chinese name for it is Ta Chui, which means "big vertebrae." In Taoist practice, we regard these bones as the main power points connecting to the arms. All the Yang energy channels of the body meet here. These points are also known as the all-tendon control points. To activate these points, sink the chest, round the scapulae, and gently pull in the chin.

The neck also plays an important role in transferring the force from the ground out to the arms. When the neck is not aligned, all the force can jam in the neck and throw off the entire structure.

RELAX THE BODY AND CALM THE MIND

There is an inverse relationship between tension and sensitivity; the more tense one is, the less sensitive one is. If one stays relaxed, the senses are more receptive to one's opponent. In martial arts, it is important to be able to sense where the opponent is weakest and where strongest. One can then yield and redirect the brunt of the opponent's force while simultaneously attacking his weak and undefended points.

By contrast, when one relies on muscular force, one's responses are often tense, insensitive, excessive, and inappropriate. One wastes one's energy confronting the opponent's strength head-on, using force against force, applying maximum effort for minimum results. This is called inefficiency.

The principle of economy in movement arises from a state of internal harmony. A mind that is at peace is not easily swayed or disturbed. This principle also plays a vital role in daily life, whether in business or in combat. If one overreacts and responds with excessive or unnecessary action, one is at a disadvantage.

The basic principle of Tai Chi is to learn how to be relaxed, calm, and mentally clear, whether doing the movements of Tai Chi, doing business, or in the midst of other activities.

The Tai Chi practitioner is likened to a tiger, walking calmly across a meadow, but with a perceptible strength. This inner state of calmness and power is enhanced by sitting meditations such as the Inner Smile and the Microcosmic Orbit, as well the standing meditations of Iron Shirt Chi Kung. Both the sitting and standing meditations require the physical structure to be aligned so there is no strain. Improper structure can cause tension and make it hard to relax.

Relaxation is sometimes confused with letting everything go to the point of collapsing the physical and mental structures. This is wrong. Tai Chi is a balance of Yin and Yang. Therefore one seeks to release any unnecessary physical and mental tension, yet at the same time stay mentally alert and physically poised. Relaxing means dropping any physical and mental preoccupation so that one enters a heightened state of receptivity and openness.

The Tai Chi Classics say, "Let go of your own will and follow the will of others." In martial arts, this means when you drop your preoccupation with your own agenda, you become empty, awake, and clear like a mirror, able immediately to perceive when the opponent is about to attack. By staying relaxed and not overreacting, you can respond instantly and appropriately, using the opponent's strength against her. Using very little effort, you can join with the Chi of the opponent's attack and guide it wherever you want. This is referred to in the Tai Chi Classics as "using only four ounces of [your] force to deflect a thousand pounds [of an opponent's force]." This skill can only be achieved by learning to relax, especially in the midst of conflict.

It is best to begin relaxation training in sitting or lying-down meditation. Because the body is immobile, it is easier to pay attention to dropping physical and mental tensions. Then you can incorporate this relaxation into your Tai Chi; the depth of relaxation experienced in meditation is carried over into a wide range of motions.

Any bodily movement involves muscular contractions and releases. It is impossible to move the structure without tensing and con-tracting whole series of muscles and tendons. The challenge in Tai Chi is to execute all the movements without tensing or tightening to the point of interfering with the energy flow, and in learning to release once the movement ceases so as to feel the newly gained Chi. This is called Wu Wei, effortlessness, using minimum effort to achieve maximum results. The Taoist Classics are full of references to Wu Wei, yet nowhere is it better demonstrated than in the gentle, flowing movements of Tai Chi.

In another part of the Tai Chi Classics, it is said, "Use mind, not force." Training the mind/eye/heart guides the Chi, moving the blood and body structure without overly depending on the muscles. The energetic expense is minimal, and internally one feels more at ease.

CLEARLY DISTINGUISH YIN AND YANG

Just as in the universe, where all manifestation is an interplay of Yin and Yang, all the movements of Tai Chi are a constant interplay of Yin and Yang. Without Yin and Yang, active and passive, there is no movement. Tai Chi practice recreates the process of cosmic expression through the sequence of movements.

The primordial state of Wu Chi is expressed in the first posture of standing still, totally centered and balanced — unmanifested. The moment the legs are separated and one begins to move, the process of Yin and Yang becomes active. In Tai Chi, Yin and Yang are primarily understood in terms of substantial (Yang) and insubstantial (Yin). This is what creates the flow of the energy.

Substantial (Yang) is a relative term in Tai Chi. It means the most active element of the moment. In terms of the legs, it can mean all or most of the weight is on one foot. In terms of the arms, it can mean one arm is in front and is discharging energy through a punch or push.

Insubstantial (Yin) refers to the other arm or leg, which is playing the supportive and stabilizing role at the moment.

In terms of advancing and sinking back, advance is Yang and sinking back is Yin. In terms of the breath, inhaling is Yin and exhaling is Yang. Raising the arms is Yang; lowering them is Yin.

The weight is constantly shifting from one leg to the other. At the same time, one hand and arm are dominant, while the other hand and arm play a supportive role. Just as with the legs, the active arm is constantly changing.

The awareness of substantial and insubstantial has a very practical purpose beyond martial arts applications. Once the body learns to move by constantly flowing from empty to full, from full to empty, it becomes apparent that these same principles can be applied to social endeavors, personal relationships, career, and politics. One discovers how to work effectively with Yin and Yang, discerning when to yield and when to advance in daily life.

COORDINATE INNER AND OUTER, MIND AND BODY

Another rule of energy circulation is that the life force follows the intention of the mind/eye/heart. The Tai Chi Classics say, "The mind intention leads and the Chi follows; the Chi leads and the body follows." So, if the intention of the mind is to move the right arm down, the life force will aid in that movement of the arm.

Moving the structure as a unit.

The Tai Chi Classics also say, "Use mind intention, not muscular force." Using the mind/eye/heart to move the Chi, one moves with a minimum of effort. In Tai Chi, one learns to move using just the right amount of energy needed to accomplish the purpose: neither too much nor too little, neither too early nor too late.

In Tai Chi, one of the basic principles is to move in coordinated continuous sequences, with all parts of the body connected and working together harmoniously. This continuous flow manifests through the physical structure as gracefulness, and through the mental structure as emotional balance and steadiness of character; this is what we call integrity. That the word integrity is rarely used nowadays in the English language reflects the imbalance of our mental and emotional structures, our lack of integration.

Attaining an integrated structure is a repair process that takes place at several levels. The most basic level is the energy flow in the body. If the life force is unable to circulate unimpeded, automatically some areas of the body will be affected with too much energy or too little. This is reflected in our thinking, our emotions, and the way we move.

As previously mentioned, emotional and mental states manifest in the physical structure. Negative emotional energy inhibits movement. Over time, emotions begin to be held in the muscles, organs, and tissues, creating tightness and restricted movement. The Microcosmic Orbit meditation opens these energy blockages by restoring energy flow.

Without mental balance and emotional stability, the practitioner of Tai Chi often struggles in vain trying to move in one piece. Without the help of meditation, it might take many years of Tai Chi practice to attain the state of mental and emotional balance that results in physical integrity.

The emotions of joy, anger, fear, sadness, worry, love, respect, and so on are the most powerful forms of energy ordinarily experienced. Fully expressing the emotions is one characteristic of a dynamic and integrated personality.

One should not be at the mercy of the emotions, however. The Fusion of the Five Elements meditation is one of the most powerful methods for regulating the emotions and recycling any excess emotional energy back into balanced life force energy. The Taoist experiences emotions fully and then allows them to flow on once the situation that provoked them is finished. Regular practice of Fusion meditation gradually creates a state of emotional balance and integrity that manifests as solidity of character and inner strength.

Through the practice of Tai Chi, this emotional state is expressed as integrated movements animated from within. Each movement becomes the manifestation of the mind, body, and spirit moving as one.

Learning to move the structure in one piece has many subtle levels of refinement. Ordinarily we move using a combination of muscles, tendons, and bones, but with little conscious emphasis on using our Chi. In Tai Chi the situation is totally reversed. As one becomes more and more acquainted with the life force through sitting, standing, and moving meditation, one is able to sense very clearly the energy moving within the limbs and trunk. One of the rules of energy circulation is that the more relaxed one is, the more easily the energy is able to circulate. For the Tai Chi practitioner, the first challenge is to relax as much as possible in each move and to feel inner calm and strength so the energy can circulate as fast as possible. The next level of subtlety is allowing the movements to flow from the life force rather than from the mechanical contraction of muscles, bones, and tendons.

The life force circulates through the body along the meridians. The prerequisite for moving animated by life force is thus to open the channels. Once again, a background in meditation provides a solid foundation for entering this subtle stage of Tai Chi. One of the results of allowing the life force to empower the movements is that the Chi can flow like a river. This enables the practitioner to move smoothly and continuously, without sudden shifts in tempo.

4

WARM-UP EXERCISES AND PREPARATION

Whether one is a student or an expert, practice is essential. A practice session can be fruitless, however, if the body is not properly prepared to handle the energy it is about to absorb. This is the main reason for these additional Tai Chi training exercises. The term *warm-up* means to activate the Chi and blood flow and invigorate their circulation throughout the body. Warm-up exercises are particularly important for areas of the body that are rarely stretched, such as the spine and the sacrum. Even a person who does muscular and aerobic workouts is still not properly prepared for the conduction of large amounts of energy. Without adequate warm-up before exercise, the muscles may also be stiff, tight, and lacking in sufficient blood supply to meet the sudden demands placed on them by strenuous activity. This is one of the major causes of athletic injury.

Following is a series of special exercises that enhance the body's receptivity and the mind's acuity to the practice of Tai Chi. The Healing Tao warm-up exercises are gentle yet effective. They are easy to learn, and you will discover they are also easy to perform.

Listen to the messages from your body as you do the various exercises. Pain is the body's warning signal that you may be overdoing it. The goal is not to go to extremes in stretching or to develop major muscles; instead, the aim is to loosen the joints and relax the muscles so the Chi and blood can flow without obstruction. Don't force yourself to your limits; less is better, especially at the beginning. If you feel any joint pain or discomfort doing any of the exercises, back off until it feels comfortable. If you still feel strain or pain, discontinue the exercise altogether.

Be especially respectful of any injuries, chronic problems, or physical limitations you may have. If you are kind and gentle to your body, it will start to trust you and relax by itself. You will find yourself starting to loosen up on a deeper level without having to force the issue. In this way you will develop naturally, gradually, and safely.

In Tai Chi, you learn to reorganize the way in which you move. In particular, you discover how to coordinate all your movements from your center and how to use the power of the waist and lower Tan Tien to move in a strong, stable, integrated way. You will see that many of the warm-up movements focus on training the waist for this reason.

WAIST LOOSENING

Backview

1. Place the feet parallel, slightly wider than shoulder width apart. Allow the arms to dangle loosely at your sides.

Begin to turn the hips from side to side. Let the arms swing naturally and easily with the momentum of the hips turning. Explore your natural and comfortable range of hip motion in this way. Don't go to extremes; just stay within your free and easy comfort zone.

2. After turning just the hips 10 or 12 times, allow the lumbar vertebrae to relax and loosen and gently twist with the motion. You should still begin the movement from the hips, but allow the lumbar vertebrae to respond.

3. Next allow the middle spine, upper back, and neck to twist gently with the movement.

Keep the shoulders loose and let the arms swing with the movement. Don't use effort to move the arms; let them be totally limp and just let the body swing them. At the same time, be aware of the gentle twisting of the knee and ankle joints as you twist the whole body. Do this at least 36 times to each side.

OPENING FROM THE DOOR OF LIFE

Backview

Door of Life

1. Begin in the same stance as for Waist Loosening. Twist to the left as in the previous exercise, initiating the movement from the hips. Let the right arm swing across the front of the torso, raising it up to head height with the palm facing away from you. At the same time, let the left arm swing around to the back and place the back of the left hand over the Door of Life point (the point on the spine opposite the navel).

2. When you reach your full extension, relax, and then extend again by loosening the lower back. Feel the gentle stretch and increased extension coming all the way from the Door of Life area, not from the shoulders. Extend in this way two or three times.

3. Twist to the right and repeat the steps as above on the right side. Repeat 9 times on each side.

WINDMILL EXERCISE: OPENING THE SPINAL JOINTS

Do each phase of this exercise very slowly and mindfully.

Outer Front Extension

1-3. Begin in the same stance as for Waist Loosening. Bring the hands together and hook the two thumbs together. Keeping the hands close to the torso, inhale and raise the arms until they are extended straight up over the head, with the fingers pointing upward. Gently stretch up in this position, extending the spine slightly backwards. You can even say "Ahhhhh" as you would when you stretch first thing in the morning.

4-5. Begin to exhale slowly and bend forward, reaching as far out in front as you can, keeping the head between the arms. Try to feel each joint of the spine releasing one by one in a wave-like motion. Bend first from the lumbar vertebra, then from the thoracic vertebra, and finally from the cervical vertebra. At this point you are bent all the way.

> "Pay attention to the waist at all times. Completely relax, and the Chi will then steam out from the Tan Tien and circulate freely through the entire body."
>
> — Song of the Thirteen Movements

6-9. Slowly straighten back up, again feeling each joint of the spine opening, from the sacrum, lumbar, thoracic, and cervical vertebrae. Keep the arms and head hanging heavily until you are back in the starting position. Repeat 3 to 5 times. Finish with the arms over the head as at the end of step **1.**

Inner Front Extension

1-3. Now do the same movements, but in reverse. Point the fingertips downward and slowly lower the arms, keeping the hands close to the torso. When the arms are completely lowered, begin to bend forward; release the head, cervical vertebra, thoracic vertebra, and lumbar vertebra, until you are bent all the way forward as at the end of step 2 of the Outer Front Extension. Feel each joint opening.

4-5. Keeping the head between the arms, start to straighten up. The arms will extend out in front as you slowly stand erect. When you finish straightening up, the arms will be straight up above the head. Repeat 3 to 5 times.

Left Outer Extension (Left Side Bending)

1. Keeping your head between your arms in the overhead position, lean to the left. You should feel a gentle stretch on the left side of the waist. Continue stretching down and to the side until you are all the way down.

2. Then circle back up on the right side until you are again standing straight with the arms overhead. Repeat 3 to 5 times.

Right Outer Extension (Right Side Bending)

Repeat the same side-bending movements as in the Left Outer Extension, but to the right. Do 3 to 5 times.

Conclusion

To finish, unhook the thumbs and let the arms slowly float back down to the sides.

TENDON TWISTING EXERCISES

In these exercises, the tendons of the wrists, elbows, and shoulders are stretched and twisted to enhance both flexibility and power. The movements should feel as if you are turning a screw into a wall.

Small Tendon Twist

1. Begin by reaching forward with both arms and twisting both hands to the outside of the body in a screwing circular motion, then around in a small circle and back forward, returning to the starting position.

While doing this, the wrists and elbows should be fully torqued to the point where you can actually hear the creaking of the tendons that are being stretched if you listen carefully. The shoulders should be relaxed and

rounded. Repeat 3 to 9 times.

2. Repeat this exercise in front, up, to both sides at the same time, and then downward in front of the body.

3. Repeat Steps 1 and 2, but reverse the direction of the tendon twist.

Large Tendon Twist

1. This is the same as the small tendon twist, but it is done in a large circle. This should only be practiced in front. Do 3 to 9 times.

2. Repeat Step 1, but reverse the direction of the tendon twist and joint opening.

HEAD ROTATIONS AND NECK JOINT OPENING

1. Let the head loll forward. Just relax and feel the weight of the head providing a gentle stretch to the back of the neck. Allow the weight of the head to provide all the loosening and stretching force; it helps you deeply relax and let go and avoids the risk of injury from overstraining.

2. Let the head roll to the right side and feel the stretch on the left side of the neck.

3. Let the head roll gently back, feeling its weight, and feel the stretch on the front of the neck.

4. Let the head roll to the left side and feel the stretch on the right side of the neck.

5. Repeat steps 1-4 twice more and then repeat 3 times in the reverse direction.

SHOULDER ROTATIONS AND JOINT OPENING

This exercise increases your scapular power. Many people, especially if they have a good strong back, develop knots of tension in the shoulders. In this exercise, the scapulae are loosened and rounded to develop the type of scapular power used by tigers and other big cats.

1. Begin by standing with the feet parallel and slightly wider than shoulder width apart. Relax the entire body, paying special attention to relaxing the shoulders, scapulae, and back. Keep the palms loosely on the front of the thighs throughout this exercise.

2. Lift the shoulders straight up.

3. Extend the shoulders forward.

4. Lower the shoulders downward.

5. Draw the shoulders back.

6. Repeat steps 1-4 8 more times.

7. Now reverse direction: raise the shoulders, draw them back, lower them, and bring them forward. Repeat 9 times.

HIP ROTATIONS

1. Stand with the feet parallel and slightly wider than shoulder width apart. Place the hands on the sides of the waist. As you perform the hip rotations, keep the head above the feet. Move slowly and easily, breathing deeply and continuously.

2. Bring the hips forward.

3. Move the hips in a big circle toward the right.

4. Now move the hips in a circle toward the back.

5. Move the hips toward the left.

6. Repeat steps 2-5 eight more times.

7. Reverse direction and repeat steps 2-5 nine times.

KNEE ROTATIONS

1. Place the feet together. Bend the knees and place the palms lightly on the kneecaps.

2. Slowly and gently rotate the knees to the left.

3. Rotate the knees to the back.

4. Rotate the knees to the right.

5. Repeat steps 1-4 eight more times.

6. Now reverse direction and repeat 9 times.

ANKLE/KNEE/HIP ROTATIONS AND JOINT OPENING

Keeping the joints open is a very important part of allowing the energy to be properly stored and available to flow into the bones. This exercise helps open the joints and flex the tendons so you do not overstress them during Tai Chi practice.

1. Raise the right leg, and with the hands on the hips, begin to rotate the right ankle 9 to 36 times clockwise, and then the same number of times counter-

clockwise.

2. Next, keeping the same leg raised, rotate the foreleg from the knee in a circular motion 9 to 36 times clockwise and then the same number of times counterclockwise.

3. Now, keeping the same leg raised, rotate the entire leg from the hip joint in a circular motion 9 to 36 times clockwise and then the same number of times counterclockwise.

4. Finally, do a front kick by bending the leg at a right angle and snapping it forward, kicking as high as you can. Be careful with this at first, working your way up so as not to accidentally harm the tendon that runs down the back of the leg.

5. Repeat these steps with the opposite leg in the same manner.

TAN TIEN HITTING

Since the Tan Tien is the major storage center for the Chi of the body, this area should be activated prior to Tai Chi practice.

1. Totally relax the arms and gracefully swing them in free fall from left to right. As you

swing to the left, the right hand comes in front of the body, with the palm hitting the navel area at the exact same time that the back of the left hand hits the Door of Life opposite the navel.

2. Then, as you swing to the

right, the left hand comes in front of the body, with the palm hitting the navel area at the exact same time as the back of the right hand hits the Door of Life.

3. Repeat 36 times to each side.

BOUNCING AND SHAKING THE JOINTS

Shaking all the joints open, when resting feel the Chi entering into the joints.

Bouncing the body can compared to a brief ride on the subway. For those of you who commute, this can be practiced on the way to work as well.

1. Just relax the body while concentrating on opening the joints, and bounce without any tension on the floor.

2. Let the vibration in the heels work its way up through the entire skeletal system from legs to spine to neck to skull. Shoulders and arms vibrate as they hang loosely by the sides of the body. To enhance this, you can hum a vowel to hear the vibration make the voice tremble as well.

3. Rest and feel the Chi entering in to the joints.

ENERGY CONNECTION EXERCISES

To the average person who is not familiar with Tai Chi, when we say that we are going to practice gathering, directing, and storing energy, the first question that may be asked is, "What energy?" Here is a series of exercises that not only prepares the body for connecting with the energy, but also enhances the mind/eye connection.

Washing the Body with Heavenly and Earth Energy

1. Stand in the Embracing the Tree position. The feet should be shoulder-and-a-half width apart, with the nine points of the feet pressed firmly against the ground. The knees are bent and torqued slightly outward with a corresponding torque in the ankles and hips. This acts to screw the body into the ground and to initiate the Earth connection. Straighten the spine by slightly tucking in the sacrum (this increases the connection to the Earth) and by tucking in the chin to connect with the Heavenly energy.

2. Reach down and forward, keeping the palms cupped upward, and slowly scoop up the Earth energy (use your imagination at first until you are sensitized) through the body. Simultaneously, feel a cool blue water-like healing sensation rising through the body at the level of the hands as you raise them up until they are fully extended above the head.

3. Turn the palms of the hands up and connect with the Heavenly energy.

4. Slowly arc the arms downward to the sides. Simultaneously, feel the Heavenly energy descend through the body at the level of the hands. The Heavenly energy may feel like a hot white fire-like expansive sensation that washes down through the body

until it reaches the ground, at which point the hands will have returned to their original position.

5. Repeat this exercise 9-36 times until you feel fully saturated with both types of energy.

Cosmic Energy Mid-Eyebrow Connection

Mid-eyebrow point

1. Repeat the stance described in Embracing the Tree for the first two steps of the first exercise described above, but facing the sun or moon. If you are facing the sun, this exercise should only be performed right at sunrise or sunset, when the light of the sun is softer and will not damage the eyes. Close and rest your eyes whenever the light feels too intense.

2. Slowly raise the palms out in front of the body with elbows slightly bent outward. Bring the

arms up to just above the level of the mid-eyebrow and make a triangle between the index fingers and thumbs of both hands, with either the sun or the moon centered within the triangle.

3. Hold this position and draw the Yang (sun) or Yin (moon) energy in through the mid-eyebrow.

4. Gather some saliva in the mouth, and mix the energy drawn in with the saliva to collect a ball of Chi energy in the mouth. This increases the

amount of saliva produced.

5. Slightly extend the neck. Swallow the saliva with a strong gulp and mentally direct it to the navel. Feel the navel warm up with the arrival of this new energy.

6. Repeat these steps from 9 to 36 times, and then close by slowly lowering the arms to the navel, placing the left hand over the right, and collecting energy by spiraling at the navel as described earlier.

> ## "Opening and closing the gates of Heaven, can you embrace the role of Feminine receptivity?"
>
> — Tao Te Ching, Chapter 10

Navel/Palm Connection

1. Place both palms approximately two inches out from the navel.

2. Slowly inhale, allowing the abdomen to fill completely with air. As this is happening, tug a "string" of energy lightly away from the navel using the centers of the palms.

3. Then, slowly exhale and feed the "string" back into the navel.

4. Repeat this 9 times, and then collect energy at the navel.

Sink Back and Push Tree Connection

1. Find a tree that gives off positive energy. Selecting the proper tree is vital, since there are trees with negative energy.

2. Then, facing the tree, sink into the Sink Back position, starting with the right leg forward. The fingers face the tree.

4. As you proceed forward into the Push, feel a connection as the energy from the fingertips shoots out and connects with the positive energy of the tree. Project out any sick or negative emotions into the tree to be healed and recycled through the earth.

5. Then, sink back and draw in the newly processed positive energy.

6. Repeat this Yin and Yang action 9, 18, or 36 times. This is particularly effective for energy sensitization in the Tai Chi form.

STRUCTURE EXERCISES

The following series of exercises build structural power and strength. Once the energy can flow, it is important that the structure is properly aligned to feed that energy into the various conduits and sites where the body needs healing and strengthening. These exercises particularly emphasize opening and developing the structure in specific areas so that the energy is able to flow properly.

Single Leg Stance with Raised Arm

The connection between Heaven and Earth through the human body is one of the main concepts in Tai Chi practice. This force can only flow if the channels are properly opened. To ensure that one side of the body is not more open than the other, and to achieve a balance between the left (Yin) side and the right

(Yang) side, this exercise allows the Heavenly force to flow in to the hand on one side of the body, and then out to the earth on the other. This creates balance and opens the channel by temporarily removing weight from the opposite leg and arm so that you double the force on one side that is ordinarily divided between the limbs.

1. Begin by standing on the right leg, with the left leg raised and bent to prevent any flow through it. Also, raise the left arm so the palm faces up, and leave the right arm relaxed at the side.

2. Keeping your balance as long as possible, draw the Heavenly force into the palm of your hand, and feel it flow through the body and then out the leg into the earth. Maintain this position for as long as possible,

building up to 3 minutes.

3. Then switch, and repeat the exercise on the opposite side. Try to do both sides of the body for equal lengths of time so as to properly balance their flow.

Dog Holding Leg: Opening the Spinal Joints

Not all the Iron Shirt exercises are taught in detail here; however, for readers who know how to do the Turtle, this is an exercise that can apply to Tai Chi.

1. From the Turtle position, take the right arm and wrap it around the right leg, with the

left arm passed between the legs and clasping the right forearm.

2. Then, slowly pulling up, arch the back and feel the current flowing from the spine, through the legs into the earth.

3. Repeat on the opposite side.

4. Finally, bending the knees a

bit more, wrap both arms around both legs and clasp the right arm at the forearm with the left hand. Again, pull up as if lifting yourself, arch the back to create a strong energy flow throughout the skeletal system.

Opening the Groin (kua)

Loosen the knees

Sink down

Don't bend the knees

Feel weight transfer down to the heel

Opening the kua is very much related to the psoas muscles (see page 32). As you do this exercise, pay close attention to deeply relaxing and lengthening the lower back (psoas) muscles.

1. Stand with your feet parallel about shoulder width apart, and place your hand on your inguinal crease.

2. Arch your back slightly, tilting your sacrum back. Then slightly tuck your sacrum forward, and sink your pelvis as if you were sitting down in a chair without bending your knees. Your hand will feel the inguinal crease deepen. Focus on the feeling of the ball and socket joint of the hip and femur opening. As the joint opens, it will feel as if it is inflating inside as it fills with Chi.

3. Feel the force transfer down into the heel. As you open and spiral out the knee joints, you will feel the same sensation of the joints opening and inflating as they fill with Chi.

4. Transfer the force to the heels and feel them open and fill with Chi.

5. Feel the force gently rebound from the Earth up through the heels to the sacrum. Feel the area between the sacrum and lumbar expand and fill with Chi. Feel the force transfer up the spine to the Door of Life as the Chi enters the spine, and feel the entire spine lengthening and straightening.

POWER EXERCISES

The previous set of exercises distinguish Tai Chi from most other forms of exercise in that the emphasis is placed on feeling the energy and opening the channels for the Chi to move. In the next series of exercises, the power is not a muscular power but is instead a practice of using the structure of the body in conjunction with the energy to produce great force.

Stork Exercise

In this exercise, the intent is to build up the power of the Achilles tendons, to strengthen the legs, and to increase the sense of balance.

1. Begin by standing on your right leg, with your left leg raised and bent (like a stork).

2. Slowly, bend your right leg

with the palms of your hands facing down and arms fully extended, lowering your entire body down to the point where your palms rest on the floor. At first, if you cannot make it all the way, just go as low as possible.

Your upper body must remain straight, with your muscles relaxed. Sink first in the groin/kua area before bending your knees.

3. Next, raise your body back up by using the force of your right leg to straighten itself out.

4. Repeat this exercise 9 or 18 times, and then do the same on your left leg, with the right on the chair.

Medicine Ball Practice

There are a few older Tai Chi practices that use props other than just the body itself. One of these is called the medicine ball, which is a heavy ball used to provide extra resistance in the practice of the Tan Tien motion. This helps develop additional strength in the lower body.

Heavy Stick Exercise

Another of the older practices with props is the heavy stick exercise. By practicing the Tai Chi motion with a very heavy wooden or iron pole over the shoulders, you increase strength in the legs and waist.

Groin Weight Lifting

Finally, an important aspect of both the higher level meditations and the Tai Chi form is the Groin Weight Lifting exercises. While the details of this exercise are fully described in my Bone Marrow Nei Kung book, it is worth mentioning here. The power of the groin and its association with the internal organs are greatly strengthened through the use of this technique. Additionally, the practice helps you better connect with the planets in the Healing form.

Sole and Heel Press

1. Place yourself in the Tai Chi front stance with the back (left) foot turned out at a 45-degree angle, with the front (right) leg bent.

2. Bend your left knee, shift your weight back and practice pressing from the sole to the heel of the back foot to send the body and Earth energy bouncing forward. It is important that while you feel the spring of the energy like a horse leaping, you still perform this slowly to let the power manifest as the weight of the body shifts from the back to the front leg.

3. Practice this from 18 to 36 times to gain a powerful forward motion.

4. Repeat on the opposite side.

5. Next, starting from the forward position, using the ball of the front foot, press down to move the body in a controlled backward motion into the sink position. Again, the ball of the foot and sole energy initiates the motion, and the rest is controlled by the slow transfer of weight from the front to the back leg.

6. Repeat this motion 18 or 36 times. Then repeat on the opposite side.

7. Finally, combine the forward and backward motions together in one powerful movement, and practice on the left and right sides for 18 or 36 times.

Low Stance Tai Chi Practice

Once you have mastered the above power exercises, it is important to optimize this power into the Tai Chi practice. This is done by performing the Tai Chi Chi Kung form with the body lower to the ground. Through bending the knees and widening the stance, the low practice of Tai Chi can enhance the ability to use the form in applications and self-defense. The increased force on the tendons of the ankles and knees further enhances your power.

Be sure to keep your body upright in your lower stance practice, and take care that your front knee does not extend beyond your toes in the forward stance.

ENERGETIC PREPARATIONS FOR TAI CHI CHI KUNG

To master Tai Chi Chi Kung, you must also master the fundamental Taoist energy practices. These practices include the Inner Smile, the Microcosmic Orbit meditation, Iron Shirt Chi Kung, and the Six Healing Sounds.

This book presents a simplified version of these practices in Appendix 1. For in-depth guidance, readers should receive personal instruction from a Certified Healing Tao Instructor. In addition, readers may refer to our books, videotapes, and audiocassettes for further information.

Although it may seem at first as if there are so many practices that there are not enough hours in the day to do them all, once you gain skill in each practice, you will find you can perform them very quickly and still get excellent results. You can then incorporate them all into your daily round of Tai Chi practice.

It is not always necessary to practice all the preparatory energetic exercises before performing each round of Tai Chi Chi Kung. You can distribute your practice throughout the day. There is no question, however, that if you precede your Tai Chi practice with a round of the Inner Smile, the Microcosmic Orbit, and Embracing the Tree, your Tai Chi will reach a more profound level.

Some people prefer to do their seated Inner Smile and Microcosmic Orbit Meditation after doing Tai Chi Chi Kung. They find that the warm-up movements, standing meditation, and Tai Chi make their bodies more open and supple, and it then becomes easier for them to relax and go deeper into their meditation. The way of the Tao is to find your own rhythm and determine what works best for you.

Having learned the warm-up and preparatory foundation practices, you are now ready to proceed on to the Tai Chi Chi Kung form itself.

5

THE TAI CHI CHI KUNG
THIRTEEN MOVEMENT FORM

Beginners and older people generally practice the Thirteen Movement Tai Chi Chi Kung form with a higher stance. As the student progresses, he or she can practice with a middle-structure stance, one that is closer to the ground, to increase strength. For martial purposes, one generally uses an extremely low stance.

INTRODUCTORY MOVEMENTS

Wu Chi Stance

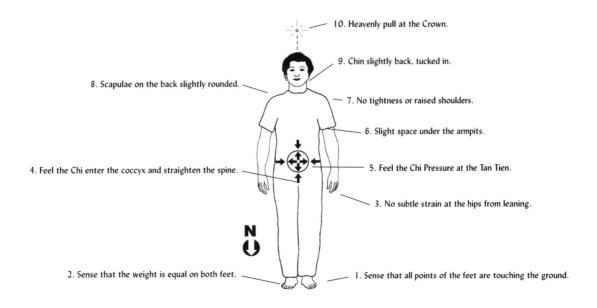

10. Heavenly pull at the Crown.

9. Chin slightly back, tucked in.

8. Scapulae on the back slightly rounded.

7. No tightness or raised shoulders.

6. Slight space under the armpits.

4. Feel the Chi enter the coccyx and straighten the spine.

5. Feel the Chi Pressure at the Tan Tien.

3. No subtle strain at the hips from leaning.

2. Sense that the weight is equal on both feet.

1. Sense that all points of the feet are touching the ground.

N

The first movement of the Tai Chi form is internal, not external. Outwardly, one is standing still, facing North. This position is related to Wu Chi, the primordial unmanifested state.

The feet are close together, but not touching at the ankles. The nine points of the feet make contact with the ground. This is the root, the connecting point with the Earth energy.

The knees are straight, but not locked. The back is straight and relaxed. No pressure, tension, or pain should be felt in the lumbar area.

The shoulders are relaxed, and the head is pulled upward at the crown. This is the Heavenly pull that draws up the Earth energy through the feet.

Feel the Heavenly pull, as if a Chi ball above your head is pulling you up. The pull also stretches the spine, allowing the energy to circulate more freely. At the same time, feel the Chi enter the coccyx and straighten the spine.

The eyes are open without strain. The focus is directly ahead, to the horizon. The chin is slightly pulled back. This subtle movement backwards opens the base of the skull area so the energy can circulate freely up to the crown and down the front.

The tongue tip is touching the palate lightly at a point that helps induce salivation.

The jaw is relaxed with the teeth lightly touching. If the jaw is biting down hard, there is tension on the sides of the head and the throat.

The throat is relaxed. Swallowing a little saliva and ex-haling gently relaxes the muscles of the neck.

The chest is relaxed and slightly hollowed. This hollowing is produced by a subtle rounding of the scapulae on the back.

If the chest is tight, one can relax it by inhaling gently without making noise and then exhaling just as quietly through the parted lips.

The breath is even and deep, expanding the abdomen.

The attention is at the navel, or at the Tan Tien, the point deeper in the body close to the kidneys. The breath penetrates to the Tan Tien, creating the sensation of a growing energy ball.

The arms are relaxed, with a hollow in the armpits, as if holding a Ping Pong ball there. The arms are not touching the body.

The palms of both hands are relaxed and the fingers are loose yet straight.

The index fingers are very slightly raised, so that energy is felt sparkling at the tips.

Smile

Smile down to the thymus gland below the neck. Allow the smile to spread to the heart and all other organs. Smile down to the navel.

Listen to the heartbeat. Follow the pulse from the heart out through the chest, shoulders, upper arms, elbows, forearms, wrists, hands, and fingers. Feel the pulse in the index and pinkie fingers.

Breathing

Become aware of the Earth energy at the feet, the Heavenly pull at the crown, and the Cosmic energy in front. Inhale gently without making noise and draw the Cosmic energy into the mid-eyebrow.

Let the Cosmic energy penetrate deeply to the lungs, spread to all the organs, and fill the soles of the feet.

When the inhalation is completed, retain the breath for a moment, without straining, and then begin to exhale gently without making noise. If a piece of paper was placed in front of the nostrils, it would not move with the air being exhaled.

Feel the Chi ball in the Tan Tien contracting and expanding with your breath.

Feel the palms and soles breathing.

OPENING TAI CHI
Preparation: Step Out

Bend at the groin (Kua).

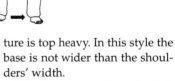

Chi Ball
Feel Chi pressure

1. With the exhalation, begin to sink down, shifting the weight onto the right leg. The sinking should originate from the hip and sacrum, sinking and folding at the groin (Kua) without much of a bend in the knees, and feel the weight transfer down the back of the knee to the heel. Sinking by simply bending the knees puts too much stress on them, resulting in swelling and injury. The arms come out slightly from the sides by sinking the chest and rounding the scapulae a little more. Rotate the hands so that the palms face back. The energy flows through the arms down to the palms and fingertips.

As the chest is sunk, the sternum moves inward, massaging the thymus gland.

The crown remains aligned with the Heavenly force, so there is no leaning to compensate for sinking down on the right leg.

When all the weight is on the right leg, inhale as you lift the left heel, keeping the big toe touching the ground.

2. Separate the left leg by brushing the ground lightly with the big toe, as if tracing a line. The separation between the two feet is roughly the width of the shoulders. This is the base. If the space between is less than shoulder width, the base is more narrow than the top, and the struc-

ture is top heavy. In this style the base is not wider than the shoulders' width.

Exhale as you place the left foot firmly touching all nine points on the ground, and shift the weight so that it is equally on both feet.

The knees remain slightly bent, but not going over the edge of the toes.

The pelvic area is open. The energy ball is in the navel area.

The spine feels stretched by the Heavenly pull up; the sacrum feels pulled down by the Earth force.

Raise the Arms

1-6. First rock slightly forward, almost imperceptibly. The nine points of the feet remain glued to the ground. Then rock back and sink the coccyx until you feel the feet connect more firmly to the earth. Allow the momentum of the Earth force rising up to the scapulae to begin raising the arms. Begin your inhalation as you start to raise the arms.

The arms, as you raise them, remain bent at the elbows. The palms of the hands and the fingers remain relaxed. There is a very subtle predominance of energy in the index fingers. The wrists are straight and relaxed so the life force can move more easily to the palms. The elbows point down, not to the sides. The distance between the arms is shoulder width. Avoid having too wide or too narrow a space between the arms.

The arms are raised mainly by internal power generated at the scapulae. The height of the raised arms does not exceed the height of the shoulders.

Two Hand Push

1-2. When the height of the arms reaches just below shoulder level, exhale slowly as you bend the elbows and sink the wrists so the palms face outward. This is done by sinking the chest and shoulders. Then, again, tilt the sacrum and sink the coccyx until you feel the nine points of the feet press firmly into the ground.

3. Feel the Earth force flow up the legs and spine.

4. Round the scapulae, tilt the sacrum skightly inward,extend the arms, slightly sink the chest, and pull in the chin. Take care that the elbows remain slightly bent and the shoulders are not raised. Feel the upward force straighten the spine.

Lower the Arms

Chi Ball

Press down with the Chi Ball

1-2. The arms are lowered through internal Chi power by relaxing the scapulae and tendon power holding the arms up. The wrists are relaxed, and the hands return to the horizontal.

The elbows remain bent, leading the movement down as if the wrists were suspended by strings. The arms should feel as if they are floating or moving in water.

3. The hands come down as far as the level of the hips, and the next movement begins.

CORE MOVEMENTS — LEFT HAND FORM

The next sequence is the core part of the Tai Chi form, which is repeated in the various directions mentioned earlier. These movements start with the left-hand form and then go through a transition into the right-hand form. At the end, there is a final series of concluding movements.

The first half of Tai Chi Chi Kung is called the Left Hand Form. The moves are in a counterclockwise progression.

Grasping the Bird's Tail: North
First Ward Off: Holding the Chi Ball

1. Begin to inhale and relax as you sink most of the weight into the right leg. Allow the life force in the Tan Tien to lead the rotation to the left (West). Avoid the mistake of turning the head and shoulders first. As the waist and

hips turn left, simply lift the left toes and allow the left foot to pivot on the heel.

2. As the waist turns, the left hand swings in a counterclockwise circle to about the height of the heart. The elbow points

down. The right hand turns palm up, as if scooping, and swings to just below the navel. The wrists and fingers in both hands are straight yet relaxed.

The distance the arms are held from the body is determined by the sinking of the chest and rounding of the scapulae. The best measure is the position of the arms in Embracing the Tree. If the wrist of the left arm was turned so the palm faces in, it would be positioned exactly at the height and distance from the body as in Iron Shirt.

The turn is made until one faces the West. The toes of the left foot are put down pointing West.

As you exhale, begin to shift about 60 percent of the weight to the left foot.

The central line of gravity running from the crown through the perineum is aligned with the left foot. This allows you to balance your structure for the next movement. If the central line of gravity is not over the left foot, the next movement will be unbalanced and off center.

Second Ward Off: Holding the Chi Ball

Side View

1. As you inhale, your mind moves the Tan Tien energy to the right. The hips follow. The upper structure moves until the hips face the Northwest. At the same time, shift 100 percent of the balance to the left foot and lift the right heel. Keep the right toes touching the ground until you feel totally poised on the left leg and until the right leg feels it can effortlessly float off the ground without disturbing the balance.

2. The right foot, which is free of weight, steps out wide to the North; at the same time, sink slightly lower into the left leg. The length of the step is determined by the length of one's leg and how far it can reach without losing the central line of gravity.

The right foot is placed so that the two feet are shoulder width apart (from left to right).

3. After the right heel touches the ground, begin to exhale as the rest of the foot comes down

with the toes pointing directly forward (North). Transfer about 50 percent of the weight to the right foot. Simultaneously with the weight being transferred, the right arm comes up from below to the height of the heart, with the palm facing toward the chest. The height, position, and angle is exactly the same as in Embracing the Tree.

The left elbow is dropped just a little so the left palm faces toward the right palm with the fingers pointing up.

The right hand holds the energy ball (now about the size of a medium cantaloupe) from the front, and the left hand holds it from the back.

Keep the chest sunk.

The center of gravity is now distributed equally over both feet.

One now faces the Northwest direction. The left foot points West, the right foot North.

4. Keeping the tailbone dropped, begin to inhale as you shift the weight on the left to the inner heel and rotate the left leg inward. The left foot also turns (45 degrees to the Northwest), pressing the ground and rotating on the heel.

5. Direct the Tan Tien force to turn to the right. As the hips begin to turn to face North, the right knee is turning outward toward the right. This creates a spiraling, screwing motion that keeps the legs rooted to the ground. When the left foot begins to turn outward, a spiraling motion is created, which begins to transfer the energy up the leg.

6. As the hip is turned to face the front, tilt the sacrum inward until you feel a solid connection to the ground. The left leg, in addition to pressing down and spiraling, begins to push forward. This push of the leg allows the spiraling energy to transfer upward to the hip and the spine.

As the left leg pushes forward, exhale and shift forward until the weight is about 70 percent on the right foot.

The arms remain in position until the left foot is finished spiraling and pushing forward. The hips face North. The spiraling energy is propelled upward by the movements of the sacral and

T-11 pumps. The force is now at C-7.

As soon as the energy reaches C-7, sink the chest and round the scapulae. The elbows remain slightly bent. The spiraling force is transferred from the scapulae to C-7 and out through the arms to the hands.

A movement simultaneous with the sinking of the chest takes place with the chin moving slightly to the back, in a recoil-

ing motion. This move adds the energy of the cranial pump and prevents the discharge of energy through the hands from whiplashing the neck. It also keeps the central line of gravity aligned with the perineum and the right leg.

Take care that the right knee does not go over the right toes and that the torso is not leaning forward, breaking the central line of gravity. Relax everything.

Rollback

1-3. Begin inhaling and feel the Earth force pulling the sacrum down, sinking slightly deeper into the right leg. The Heavenly force produces a corresponding counterpull up. The right leg then begins to push into the earth and the left knee bends, moving the structure back.

The feet remain exactly where they are. Straighten the right wrist and extend the fingers to point forward, so the palm no longer faces the body but now faces the left side. The left arm

rotates the hand so the palm faces up. As you sink back, bring the left hand under the right hand and pass it along the underside of the right arm (but without touching the right arm) until it is just under the right elbow.

Take care to keep the chest sunk and the arms rounded. Don't allow the right arm to collapse so it becomes closer to the body.

4-6. Exhale as your mind directs your Tan Tien Chi to turn to the left. The hips turn slightly

to the right as your Tan Tien and waist turn left, creating a slight torque. The upper structure of the spine and arms remains exactly as they are. As you turn, extend the spiraling into the right arm so the right hand rotates until the palm is turned toward the face.

The most common mistake in rolling back is turning the head and eyes first, followed by the shoulders and finally the hips. In such a sequence, the spine is twisted when the head and shoulders turn.

"Full and empty should be clearly distinguished."

– Tai Chi Classics

Two Hand Press

Side View

1. When the left turn of the hips reaches about 60 percent of your limit, without twisting the spine, begin the left arm movement.

Inhale as the left arm describes a scooping circle with the palm up. The hand never goes over the level of the ear when circling above.

2-3. As the left hand describes the upper part of the circle, the Tan Tien Chi starts to direct the hips to turn back toward the North. These two moves are synchronized so the heel of the left hand completes the circle and comes to press on the heel of the right hand at the same instant that the hips complete their turn to face the North. The left hand serves to support the right wrist and to reduce the potential for injury when push-ing forcefully into an opponent.

4-6. Most of the weight is on the left foot throughout the previous moves. Once the hands meet and the hips face North, one begins to spiral and transfer the energy forward to discharge it through the hands.

A common mistake is to begin transferring the weight to the right foot before aligning the hips to face directly forward. The spiraling energy is then dissipated before it reaches the hands, and the move is totally ineffective.

The spiraling of the energy begins as you exhale and press the left foot to the ground. The left knee turns outward to the left side. As the left leg begins to push forward, the right knee spirals outward to the right. When the spiraling energy reaches the sacrum, align and activate the sacral pump by tucking slightly in. As the left leg push continues and the spiraling energy reaches the T-11, add the force of the T-11 pump by curving and pushing a little at T-11. Eventually the force will reach the C-7; the pump at C-7 is activated by sinking the chest and rounding the scapulae.

As the force is transferred through the arms and begins to reach the hands the right hand twists clockwise while the left hand twists counterclockwise, like opening a jar. The last movement is pulling the chin back to activate the cranial pump.

About 70 percent of the weight is now on the right foot. Take care that the right knee is not extended beyond the right toes.

"The movement is rooted in the feet, developed in the legs, directed by the waist and expressed through the hands and fingers. From the feet to the legs to the waist should be one unbroken Chi flow."

— Tai Chi Classics

Two Hand Push

1-5. Inhale, relax and sink back on the left foot. The sacrum is pulled down once again, and the Heavenly pull stretches the spine up. The right leg in front begins to push into the earth, moving the structure back.

Take care not to bounce up; the body moves level to the ground.

Maintaining their connection, both hands turn palm down. Start to separate the hands by drawing the left hand lightly over the top of the right hand.

Continue to separate the hands until they are shoulder width apart. Sink the elbows while keeping the hands in line with the forearms, bringing the palms to face the front. The shape and position of the hand relative to the forearm in this movement and throughout the form is referred to as Fair Lady's Hand. Fair Lady's Hand is a perfect blending of Yin and Yang: the fingers are straight, but not too straight, relaxed but not collapsed, separated but not too far

apart. The wrists are bent neither forward nor backward, a position which could be described as regal or elegant.

Although the optical illusion is that the elbows are contracting and coming closer to the chest, this is not the case. The chest remains sunk and the scapulae rounded.

The correct height of the hands is about level with the ears. This is also called "protecting the head."

6-9. After sinking back, the next move is pushing forward. Once again, begin to exhale as the left leg presses down into the earth. As the energy spirals upward, activate the sacral, T-11, and C-7 pumps as previously explained. Feel as if the body is

going to jump upward, but take care not to bounce.

As the energy reaches C-7 and spreads to the arms, refrain from pushing from the elbows. Let the energy from the scapulae provide the main force. Add the energy of the cranial pump

toward the end of the move by pushing the chin back.

When the energy reaches the palms and spreads to the fingers, the tendon power stretches the fingers, but the centers of the palms remain relaxed. Take care that the center of the palms does not come out so that the fingers bend back.

The wrists remain perfectly straight in alignment with the forearm. A common mistake is to bend the wrists backward. In a combat situation, such a position is vulnerable and could injure the wrists by allowing an opponent to bend the hands totally back. The left arm and hand twist clockwise and the right arm spirals counterclockwise.

Single Whip: South
First Twist: Shift and Pivot

1-3. Inhale as you sink back into the left leg. The elbows straighten (but not completely; always keep a slight bend in the elbows and knees to allow the Chi to flow through the joints) so the palms can face down to the ground. The arms are parallel to the ground.

4. Begin to exhale as your mind directs the Tan Tien Chi to turn to the left. The hip follows the turning of the Chi. The spine, shoulders, and head are turned by the turning of the hip; they do not turn independently.

5-6. During the turning of the hip, allow the right leg and foot, which are in front, to be pulled along and turned by the hip. Simply lift the right toes and

pivot the foot on the heel. Continue turning until the hip cannot turn anymore (the hips will turn about 90 degrees to face West). The right foot pivots, toes pointing West, then the sole is put back on the ground. It is important to keep the left leg stable as you turn the hip. Allow the left hip joint to rotate and close as much as possible as you turn.

7-8. Then release the lower back and turn the waist independently of the hips, twisting the lumbar vertebrae until the arms face Southwest. Exert a slight counter-twist to the right with the hips to keep them stationary as the waist and upper body twist to the left. Continue the twist with the upper spine

and shoulders until the arms face South. A common mistake is to keep turning the head, eyes, and shoulders after the hip has ceased to turn, so the spine is twisted.

Turning the waist produces a coiling force in the left leg, like a rubber band coiled around a stick in one direction. If the rubber band is attached to the end of a stick that is wound, when the stick is released, it spins as the energy is released from the coil of the rubber band. The left leg is the rubber band, and the arms are the stick at the end. The movement winds up the force in the leg and releases it up the leg, through the spine, and out the arms.

Second Twist: Forming the Beak

1-2. When you have reached your maximum turn to the left, inhale as you press the left leg to the ground and shift to the right. As you shift, the you will allow the elbows to bend slightly.

3. Once you have shifted weight to the right, exhale as the hips turn toward the right. The coiled energy in the left leg is thus transferred to the right leg. All the weight is now on the right leg.

4. As the hips are turning right, the right arm bends at the elbow, and the right hand forms into a beak. The thumb and the pinkie finger touch, and all the other fingers press around them. The beak is an offensive weapon for pecking forcefully or for grabbing. If the pinkie finger is not protected by the other fingers, it can easily be broken.

5-7. Simultaneously, as the right arm contracts and forms the beak, the left hand comes under the right elbow in a scooping motion. A common mistake is to move the right arm tightly close to the body and bring the left arm almost touching the abdomen. The sinking of the chest and the circularity of the arms is lost. The transfer of the force coiled in the leg then is broken at the scapulae.

The wrist of the right (beak) hand is held at a height between the shoulder and the bottom of the ear.

> ## "All the joints of the body should be connected, without allowing even the slightest break."
>
> – Tai Chi Classics

Third Twist: Releasing the Beak

1-2. Inhale and begin releasing the coiled energy in the right leg by directing the Tan Tien Chi to turn the hip to the left. As the energy is released and the hip is turned left, the left foot pivots on the big toe. All the weight

remains poised on the right leg.

3. As the force uncoils, it travels up the spine and is released through the right arm and the beak.

The beak is extended to the West, keeping the elbow slightly

bent at the end of the movement. If the elbow were completely straightened or locked, it would be very difficult to retract the arm if it were grabbed, and the elbow could easily be dislocated.

Reaching to Heaven

1-2. Once the coiled energy has been released through the right arm and all the weight is on the right foot, the left leg is free to step out wide.

The central line of gravity running from crown through perineum should be positioned directly over the right foot, so that you are completely balanced on the right leg, and the step with the left leg is smooth. If not, the step has to be made quickly before falling.

The left foot aims for an angle

45 degrees to the left from where the right foot is positioned. Once again, if one is working in a room, the leg would be placed toward the corner of the room with the foot facing the wall of the room.

The heel of the left foot touches the ground first. The feet, if viewed from above, are at a 90 degree angle to each other. The right foot is still pointing to the West and the left to the South.

3. Exhale as the weight is shifted so it is equally distrib-

uted between the two feet.

Simultaneously with the shifting, the toes of the left foot come down, pointing directly South, bringing the other eight points of the foot into firm contact with the ground.

4-5. At the same time as the shifting, the left arm describes an arc with the palm facing the body; the left hand rises to the height of the face, about a forearm's length away from the face. Make certain to keep both shoulders relaxed and both elbows pointing toward the ground. The left hand is opened palm upward (reaching toward heaven), and the right hand retains the beak.

When the weight is equal on both feet, the right arm is positioned over the right leg and the left arm is over the left leg. The groin is open, and the hips face Southwest.

Single Hand Push

1-2. Inhale and turn the right foot to face 45 degrees toward the Southwest, pivoting on the heel. The mind then directs the Tan Tien Chi to turn left. The hips follow.

3-4. Exhale as the right foot presses into the ground and begins to spiral the energy up the right leg.

5-6. The right leg begins to push into the ground, moving the hip to face South and spiraling the energy up into the hips and spine. The sacral, T-11, and C-7 pumps are activated as the energy spirals up. The chest is sunk and the scapulae rounded, transferring the force out the left arm. Finally, the force of the cranial pump is added by moving the chin back in a recoil action.

The elbow of the left arm is kept slightly bent, so the wrist of the left hand is not bent. Make sure the weight is 70 percent in the front leg. Open the groin of the front leg, and let your connection to the ground be stronger and down the inside of the front leg.

This completes the core movements of Tai Chi Chi Kung I. The sequence Grasping the Bird's Tail and Single Whip are repeated five more times. In each of the next two repetitions, the direction is changed by 90 degrees counterclockwise.

Grasping the Bird's Tail: West

After completing the above sections, two more repetitions of Grasping the Bird's Tail and Single Whip are performed, ending with a Single Whip to the North.

Transition Movement: Sink Back and Protect the Chest

1-3. Inhale and sink down on the right leg. At the same time, rotate the left wrist so the palm faces the body. The

proper measure for this move is the Embracing the Tree arm position. Simultaneously, the right arm comes down

to the side near the thigh, relaxing the fingers.

The chest remains sunk and the scapulae rounded.

First Ward Off: Holding the Chi Ball

1-4. Exhale and push forward with the right foot until the weight is about 60 percent on the left leg. The left

hand begins to turn palm facing down. The right hand comes scooping from below. Simultaneously the Tan Tien

Chi turns to the left side, turning the hips. Take care that the hips turn the spine, shoulders, and head.

> "Your posture should be erect yet relaxed, able to meet an attack from the eight directions."
>
> – Tai Chi Classics

Second Ward Off: Holding the Chi Ball

From here on, the set repeats itself exactly as before, but with a new directional orientation. The rest of Grasping the Bird's Tail is now performed facing the West, followed by Single Whip to the East.

Rollback

Press

Sink Back

Push

Single Whip: East

> "Appear like a hawk seizing a rabbit;
> your spirit is like a cat catching a rat."
>
> – Tai Chi Classics

Grasping the Bird's Tail: South

Do another repetition of the Core Movements; this time, perform Grasping the Bird's Tail to the South, followed by Single Whip to the North.

> "Seek the straight from the curved. Store energy first,
> and then issue it. . . . To withdraw is to attack,
> and to attack is to withdraw."
>
> – Tai Chi Classics

Single Whip: North

You have now concluded the Left Hand Form.

CORE MOVEMENTS: RIGHT HAND FORM

Up to this point, all the movements have been done turning to the left side. With the transition, all the movements are done turning to the right side.

Transition to Right Hand Form: Holding the Baby

1-2. The left and right arms drop as the Tan Tien Chi turns the hips to the right (Northeast). Both palms turn up.

Grasping the Bird's Tail: North
First Ward Off

In this transition movement into the Right Hand Form, there is no First Ward Off movement. In all subsequent repetitions of Grasping the Bird's Tail, you perform First Ward Off as in the Left Hand Form, but with left and right hands and feet reversed.

Second Ward Off

1-3. Holding the Chi ball. The right arm describes a circle, not going over the level of the right ear. The left arm comes up to the position of Ward Off. The weight shifts at the same time to the left leg, which is in the front. The hips turn to face forward as the arm movement is completed. The palms are holding an energy ball in front. The position is the Second Ward Off. This set continues exactly as outlined for the Left Hand Form, but with the opposite hands.

Rollback

Press

Push

> "Storing energy is like drawing a bow;
> releasing energy is like shooting an arrow."
>
> – Tai Chi Classics

Single Whip: South

Grasping the Bird's Tail: East

Sink Back to Protect Chest   **First Ward Off**

> "The energy should be slightly reserved and stored by rounding so that there will always be a surplus."
>
> – Tai Chi Classics

Second Ward Off

Rollback

Press

Sink Back   Push

Single Whip: West

> "The energy appears relaxed,
> but is actually powerful and firmly rooted."
>
> — Tai Chi Classics

Grasping the Bird's Tail: South

"The mind leads, and the body follows."

— Tai Chi Classics

Single Whip: North

"Always remember that when one part moves, all parts move;
when one part is still, all parts are still."

– Tai Chi Classics

CONCLUDING MOVEMENTS

The concluding movements close the Tai Chi form. After one has generated and absorbed all the surrounding energy, it is important to collect the energy in the Tan Tien for storage.

Cross Hands

1. Inhale as you shift the weight back to the left leg. At the same time, raise the hands above the head and in front of the body so the palms face out and up, with the fingers pointing toward each other.

2. Circle the arms out to the sides. As they pass shoulder level, exhale as you raise the right toes, step straight back with the right leg, and touch the toes down shoulder width from the left foot with the foot facing North.

3. The two hands continue to scoop down in a large circular motion to the sides. At the same time, shift all the weight to the right leg.

4. Inhale and continue scooping the arms inward until the wrists cross in front of the navel with the palms facing up, collecting all the surrounding energy through the arms into the navel. Simultaneously step in with the left leg and place the left foot next to the right foot. The knees should still be bent.

5. Shift the weight to the middle so it is equally divided between the two legs. The hands, still crossed at the wrists, continue rising in front of the body until they reach throat level.

Closing Tai Chi: Hun Yuan Stance

1. Separate the two hands, palms up, to shoulder width apart.

2. Then begin to exhale as you turn the palms to face downward and slowly lower the arms.

3. As the hands approach waist level, the legs slowly straighten, returning to full standing height. Finally, bring the arms back to the sides in the same position as at the beginning of the form, in Wu Chi stance.

Stand for a minute, breathing

naturally. Feel the energy you have generated through performing Tai Chi Chi Kung. Let all the channels open and just allow the energy to flow freely though the entire body. Feel that there is one connected river of Chi in the body, with no obstruc- tions or blockages anywhere. Take time to enjoy this sensation with full awareness.

Collecting Energy

At the end, as with all the practices of the Tao, collect the energy by placing both hands over the navel and mentally spiraling 36 times in a clockwise direction, followed by 24 times in a counterclockwise direc-

tion (women spiral 36 times counterclockwise and 24 times clockwise). If you wish, you may shorten the collecting by spiraling 9 times out and 9 times in.

"Relax the belly, and the Chi will penetrate to the bones."

– Tai Chi Classics

Summary: Components of the Tai Chi Chi Kung Form

The following is an outline of the Tai Chi Chi Kung movements. It is helpful to learn the names of the different movements to help you remember the sequence.

INTRODUCTORY MOVEMENTS

Wu Chi Stance
- Smile
- Breathe in Energy

Opening Tai Chi
- Preparation: Step Out
- Raise Arms
- Two Hand Push
- Lower the Arms

CORE MOVEMENTS: LEFT HAND FORM

Grasping the Bird's Tail: North
- First Ward Off: Holding the Chi Ball
- Second Ward off: Holding the Chi Ball
- Rollback
- Two Hand Press
- Two Hand Push

Single Whip: South
- First Twist: Shift and Pivot
- Second Twist: Forming the Beak
- Third Twist: Releasing the Beak
- Reaching to Heaven
- Single Hand Push

Grasping the Bird's Tail: West
- Transition Movement: Sink Back and Protect the Chest
- First Ward Off: Holding the Chi Ball
- Second Ward Off: Holding the Chi Ball
- Rollback
- Two Hand Press
- Two Hand Push

Single Whip: East

Grasping the Bird's Tail: South

Single Whip: North

CORE MOVEMENTS: RIGHT HAND FORM

Transition to Right Hand Form: Holding the Baby

Grasping the Bird's Tail: North
- Second Ward Off: Holding the Chi Ball
- Rollback
- Two Hand Press
- Two Hand Push

Single Whip: South

Grasping the Bird's Tail: East

Single Whip: West

Grasping the Bird's Tail: South

Single Whip: North

CONCLUDING MOVEMENTS

Cross Hands

Closing Tai Chi (Hun Yuan Stance)

Collecting Energy

6
Sequence for Home Practice

The sequence for home practice is divided into three levels: beginner, intermediate, and advanced. Having a solid foundation in the beginning stages ensures a better understanding of the intermediate and advanced levels.

BEGINNING STAGE
Meditation and Chi Kung for Tai Chi

Tai Chi Chi Kung is a continuation of the different meditation practices (Inner Smile, Microcosmic Orbit, the Fusion practice, etc.). It is important to support Tai Chi with regular meditation practice. Tai Chi is also a continuation of Iron Shirt Chi Kung, so it is vital to practice the different positions of Iron Shirt, especially Embracing the Tree and Golden Turtle Submerging in Water.

Wu Chi Stance

Dedicate some time to practicing the first position of Tai Chi, known as the Wu Chi Stance. This requires simply standing still and allowing the body to relax as much as possible.

Standing in this position, make sure there is no leaning in any direction. The Heavenly pull

is the best guide for this. The moment one leans, the pull from above is decreased or cut off. Experiment with this, and your experience will tune you into the best structural connection.

Stand still for several minutes, allowing the body to relax as much as possible in the posture. Any pain that begins to develop in any area is an excellent indication of misalignments in the Wu Chi stance.

Feet

Become aware of the nine points of the feet touching the ground and check that the weight is equally distributed on both feet. Make sure the toes are relaxed and not contracted as if gripping the floor.

Knees

Move the awareness to the knees. Check to see that the knees are slightly bent. This assures that the weight of the body does not jam up in the knees, as it would if the knees were hyperextended backward as if locked in place. Locking the knees puts too much of the load-bearing work onto the knees; it affects the lower back, as well as cutting off the Chi and blood circulation from the rest of the body.

As you slightly rock the feet from the heel to the sole, gradually feel the weight drop into the feet and away from the knees. The weight should be slightly heavier on the heel, sending the force down the back of the knee rather than the front.

Spinal Cord

Move the awareness up the legs to the back, and check that there is no strain in the area of the lumbar vertebrae due to a tilted pelvis. Make sure the spine is not slumped forward.

Continue moving the awareness up the back to the shoulders. Check that the shoulders are not tense or raised upward. Continue directing the attention upward to the base of the skull and make sure the chin is slightly pushed back, creating a feeling of openness.

Head

Check that the head is not leaning forward. Feel a slight pull upward at the crown as the Heavenly force draws up the Earth force. Relax as much as possible; let the Heavenly pull hold you suspended and stretch the spine.

You may need to adjust the angle of the head very slowly. Notice the way the energy flows from the soles of the feet to the crown when the Heavenly pull is strong.

Eyes

Keep the eyes open and relaxed. Focus the vision directly ahead, not on the floor or the sky. Then, become aware of the corners of the eyes being relaxed by a very subtle inner smile.

Jaws

Relax the jaws and make sure they are not closed tightly. The back molars should not be pressing down hard. Keep the tongue lightly touching the palate at a comfortable angle that does not produce a lot of saliva.

Corners of the Mouth

The corners of the mouth are slightly raised by an inner smile. Relax the muscles of the neck and throat as much as possible. Swallowing a little saliva helps relax the muscles.

Chest

Move the awareness to the sternum. If there is tension, inhale slowly without straining further and slowly exhale through the mouth until there is no more air in the lungs.

Lower Abdomen

Check that the muscles of the lower abdomen are relaxed, expanding with each inhalation and contracting with each exhalation naturally and effortlessly.

Anus and Perineum

Place the attention at the anus, and maintain a very subtle contraction. It is important that this anal contraction not be forceful, as that would generate strain throughout the torso. The contraction is rather the result of good muscular tone in the perineum.

Armpits

Bring the awareness to the armpits. Leave enough space under the armpits for each to hold a Ping Pong ball.

Palms

Allow the center of the palms to be fully relaxed and the fingers to hang freely.

Points to Observe

While doing the complete Tai Chi Chi Kung set, pay attention to each of the following points:

- The center of gravity is mainly centered around the Tan Tien.
- The Heavenly pull is always maintained.
- The speed is even throughout.
- The movements flow continuously without jerks or sudden changes.
- The breath is even and never held.
- Natural abdominal breathing is maintained throughout.
- The chest is lightly sunk and the scapulae rounded.
- The nine points of the feet always touch the ground fully whenever one is not stepping.
- Yin and Yang, fullness and emptiness, are distinguished in each step.
- The hips guide the movements of the torso.

- The structure of the back is not broken when sinking down.
- The elbows always point to the ground.

During each round of practice, select one of the points above for special emphasis. Stay with that point until you feel you have it mastered, and then select a different point for emphasis.

Holding the Position

Begin the Tai Chi set. Stop on each position and hold it while you check the following:

- Is there a pull at the crown?
- Is the spine aligned?
- Is there any leaning?
- Is the center of gravity around the lower abdomen?
- Does the knee extend beyond the edge of the toes?
- Are the nine points of the feet making contact with the ground?
- Is the position solid or unstable?
- Are the eyes looking ahead?
- Is the breathing relaxed?

Take your time with each posture. Gradually increase the length of time you hold each posture, starting at 30 seconds and building up to five minutes. Watch for developing pains and strains; they may give you an indication of subtle misalignments.

INTERMEDIATE LEVEL

When all the points covered in the beginning level have been integrated into the Tai Chi form, one can continue the refining process at the intermediate level.

Feel the muscles separating from the bones.

Experience deep relaxation in the meditation practice to the point where you feel the muscles separating from the bones. This level of relaxation allows a far more efficient flow of life force than anything previously experienced. Bring that level of relaxation into the movements of Tai Chi.

Guide the form with the mind/eye/heart and Chi flow.

As a continuation of moving in deep relaxation, allow the Tai Chi movements to be guided primarily by the mind and Chi, and less by the muscular contraction that is typically used in the beginning level.

Maintain a smooth and even tempo.

Observe the rate at which the movements are done at the beginning of the set and aim at having that same flow in the last movements of the set. Since the emphasis here is on the gracefulness of your Tai Chi, the rate must be uniform throughout the form.

Concentrate on energy discharge.

Begin by separating each element of the movement and feel the energy being transferred at each stage. Practicing with slow movements, one is able to feel the exact position of the energy at each stage.

Regulate the size of the step.

The best guide is marking the spot where you begin the set. If the steps are always equal, you will finish the set on the same spot at which the form began, or very near it. Even steps also place you facing the exact direction of each transition.

Regulating the measure of your step depends on the length of the legs. If the steps are too short, one usually ends up with the knees extending over the edge of the toes, which puts too much weight on the knees and causes knee pain. If the step is too wide, the center of gravity is lost during the step.

Check for leaning.

The specific signs are:
- One shoulder is higher than the other.
- The hands are not equal when pushing or turning.
- The hip bone and sacrum are tilted to one side during sinking back.
- You lean forward during push and ward off.
- You lean back during sinking motions.

ADVANCED PRACTICE

When all the points covered in the beginning and intermediate levels have been assimilated into the form without having to think or check each item, one is considered to have reached an advanced level of Tai Chi practice. Here are the important points to follow at this level:

1. The calmness of mind cultivated through meditation leads to an absence of random thoughts. Aim at maintaining that state during Tai Chi.

2. Sense the energy flow at each stage of the movements. Let the mind dissolve into energy and movement.

3. Maintain even breathing throughout. Inhale during the Yin phase of each movement (sinking back, turning, etc.); exhale during the Yang phase (Ward Off, push, Single Whip, etc.). Eventually the coordinated inhalations and exhalations should be done automatically and without conscious effort.

4. Keep your gaze steady without excessive blinking or looking around. The eyes are the mirror of the mind and the spirit. Keep your eyes relaxed yet alert.

5. Maintain total concentration on the movements without being disturbed by sounds.

6. Acquire muscular relaxation and suppleness, yet be able to discharge energy instantly.

7. Move and step noiselessly.

8. Remain centered at the Tan Tien throughout the set.

Part Two

7

The Yin and Yang Inner Smile Form

YIN AND YANG IN TAI CHI CHI KUNG

The inseparability, interpenetration, and dynamism of Yin and Yang are expressed by the Tai Chi symbol. The Tai Chi symbol represents movement: the Yang pushing the Yin and the Yin drawing in the Yang. The original Chinese characters for Yin and Yang depicted the dark and sunny sides of a mountain respectively. Their qualities are relative; the Yang side is hot, bright, and dry, in contrast to the Yin side, which is cold, dark, and wet.

As profound as it may be, this symbol is no more than a symbol; the concept of Yin and Yang is valueless unless it can be related to the continuous movement of the dance of life.

The Tai Chi symbol.

The changes of Yin and Yang maintain the circle of balance in nature; night follows day, the moon follows the sun, winter follows summer. When the winter gets too cold, we know the warmer spring is coming. When the summer gets too hot, we know the cool autumn weather is near.

Similarly, in Tai Chi Chi Kung, the concept of Yin and Yang is given physical reality. Tai Chi is a way of experiencing Yin and Yang consciously. Certain movements are more characteristically Yin, while others are more Yang.

Specific physical interpretations of Yin and Yang include:

Yin	Yang
Earth	Heaven
Inhaling	**Exhaling**
Drawing in energy	Discharging energy
Sinking down	Rising up
Retreating	Advancing
Closing	Opening
Lowering	Raising
Bending	Straightening
Contracting	Expanding
Receptive	Active
Supportive	Dominant
Yielding	Firm
Bottom	Top
Storing	Releasing
Inner	Outer
Soft	Hard
Defense	Attack

As indicated by the Tai Chi symbol, every movement in Tai Chi Chi Kung is a particular combination of Yin and Yang. The more Yang, the less Yin; the more Yin, the less Yang. The sequence of movements in Tai Chi is choreographed such that the relative proportions of Yin and Yang are constantly changing. A situation that could be initially characterized as primarily Yin transforms itself, through the flow of the movements, into a situation that could be described as primarily Yang by gradually increasing the Yang and correspondingly decreasing the Yin.

Although the proportions of Yin and Yang are constantly changing, we conventionally describe the movements in terms of the pole we are moving toward. Hence the changes described in the previous sentence would be expressed thus: Greatest Yin to Lesser Yin to Lesser Yang to Greatest Yang to Lesser Yang to Lesser Yin to Greatest Yin. This cycle continues to repeat itself throughout the Tai Chi Chi Kung Form.

Relaxation and Activity

Relaxation is the key to being able to distinguish Yin and Yang. Relaxation is the foundation of activity. It is also crucial to absorbing Chi. Smiling, as taught in the practice of the Inner Smile, is an extremely effective relaxation technique. It is important to begin the Tai Chi Chi Kung form with a smile and continuously smile throughout.

The smile begins in the eyes and spreads across the face, slightly lifting the corners of the mouth. The smile is then directed to the organs, particularly the heart and kidneys.

Smiling to the joints helps open them, which results in freer movement. Smiling to the muscles relaxes them, separating them from the bones, which results in a smoother Chi flow. Smiling to the bones draws energy into them. The goal of Tai Chi Chi Kung is to use the mind to absorb, transform, and direct Chi. The Inner Smile sets the stage for accomplishing this goal.

The Inner Smile.

Earth and Heaven

It is useful to recall the image of the tree in beginning the Tai Chi Chi Kung form, as it depicts an ideal arrangement for absorbing energy. The roots are sunk deep in the ground, absorbing the Earth force; the trunk is straight, reaching up to absorb the Heavenly force; the leaves spread out to absorb the Cosmic force.

Absorbing the Earth force.

To initiate the Tai Chi Chi Kung form, lightly tuck in the sacrum so the coccyx aligns with the spine, and the force is felt at the lumbar region. This subtle movement presses the nine points of the feet more firmly into the ground. Lightly and gradually rock the feet from the sole to the heel until you feel the force move up the heel to the hip and spine. Feel the bubbling springs activate as the Earth energy draws up into the Bubbling Spring point in the middle of the foot, and then travels up the legs, and into the spine at the coccyx.

The Earth energy initiates a wavelike motion in the spine. Once the energy reaches the scapulae, the Chi causes the arms to rise to shoulder height. As the chest sinks and the chin is pulled in, the energy continues up through the cervical spine to the crown. As the crown, the highest part, is extended up, a connection is made with the Heavenly force. An upward pull is experienced, so the whole skeletal frame feels as if it were suspended from above.

Throughout the form, maintain the connection with the Three Forces. Feel rooted to the earth, and yet pulled toward the heavens. The fingers are spread, gently moving like leaves swaying in a breeze, as you feel the Cosmic force. The Cosmic force is experienced as an ocean of Chi all around you.

Absorbing the Heavenly force.

Energy is drawn during the Yin phase of movement. The process of emptying, which is considered to be Yin, creates more space to be filled. Breathing is an example of this process. The end of an inhalation is fully Yin on the outside of the body. At this point the lungs are fully Yang on the inside, and completely expanded. As the hot Yang air is expelled, the outside of the body becomes more Yang, while the insides are emptied, becoming Yin, with an increased potential to absorb air. Softly absorb energy into the palms and soles; absorb gently as if you were pulling a silken thread.

The Earth force is cool and enters through the most Yin part of the body, the feet; it is therefore considered Yin. The Heavenly force is hot and enters through the most Yang part of the body, the head; it is therefore considered Yang. Humanity is between these two forces and responsible for harmonizing them.

As Yin and Yang energies are drawn in and combined and blended in the Tan Tien, they are transformed into a highly usable Chi that can nourish the entire being as it is circulated in the Microcosmic Orbit.

Harmonizing Heaven and Earth force at the Tan Tien.

Emptiness and Fullness in the Legs

One of the most important features of Yin and Yang in Tai Chi Chi Kung is awareness of emptiness and fullness. Throughout the performance of the Core Movements, you shift weight back and forth between the right and left legs. The weight-bearing leg is the full leg; it is the more Yang or active leg because it is doing the majority of the work in supporting the weight. Similarly, the empty leg is the one that is bearing little or none of the body weight; it is more relaxed, Yin, empty of tension.

Keep in mind an important law of Yin and Yang: nothing is entirely Yin or entirely Yang. Yang always contains some Yin, and Yin always has some Yang in it. Therefore, full and empty refer to the predominant Yin or Yang quality of the leg. For example, the full leg is anywhere from 51 to 99 percent Yang; yet while Yang may predominate, that leg is still anywhere from 1 to 49 percent Yin.

Once you begin to move, you must clearly distinguish Yin and Yang. The full leg is the power leg, as it releases the stored energy like a bow releasing an arrow. As you release, the full leg becomes empty, and the empty leg, by being Yin and receiving the body weight as you shift, becomes Yang or full. The *Tao Te*

Ching expresses this idea in the verses, "That which would straighten must first be bent; that which would fill must first be empty."

Emptiness and Fullness in the Arms

The arms are always changing from empty to full in a similar way. One arm is always dominant and substantial, while the other is supportive, receptive, and insubstantial. The full arm is always opposite the full leg. For example, when the weight is predominantly on the left leg, the right arm is the full arm.

Functional Opposition

The full and empty sides change during each movement. For example, in the movement of Push (in the left-hand-side form), initially the right leg is forward and weighted. As you shift the weight back to the left leg, the right hand becomes the dominant hand, and the left hand should be slightly more relaxed, playing a receptive and supportive role at first. As you start to shift forward, the right hand is dominant at the beginning of the Push, but as the right leg begins to fill up with the body weight, the right hand should proportionately relax as the left hand becomes dominant.

This idea is illustrated in the way a right-handed baseball pitcher throws a ball. He first winds up and shifts his weight back into the right leg, storing energy. Then he shifts weight forward into his left leg and releases the ball.

Another example is in how you swing the arms when you walk or run. As one leg comes forward, the opposite arm swings forward as a counterbalance. Functional opposition occurs throughout the Tai Chi Chi Kung form, serving to balance upper and lower, left and right.

Functional opposition is a major technique of keeping Yin and Yang balanced in Tai Chi.

Avoid the Fault of Double-Weightedness

When you fail to distinguish clearly between Yin and Yang, emptiness and fullness, this is called double-weightedness. Double-weightedness can happen in several ways. The first is when both arms try to be Yang at the same time, or when the weight falls evenly on both legs at the same time. (During the Core Movements this is a fault; during the Opening Movements, it is not a fault, as you are expressing Yin and Yang in terms of up and down, expansion and contraction.) When the weight is divided 50-50 between the feet, it becomes more difficult to shift quickly to one side or the other. Many people have experienced this sensation in sports such as tennis and racquetball, when they were caught "flat-footed" and were unable to respond quickly.

The second way double-weightedness occurs is when both the upper and lower body on one side are both Yang or both Yin. To use the example of the baseball pitcher again, you never see a right-handed pitcher step forward with his right leg as he throws. Try it, and you will see how awkward this is. To prevent this type of double-weightedness, always make sure that when you want power in the right arm, the weight shifts to the left leg, and vice-versa. Similarly, when you want the left arm to be yielding or empty, the right leg should also be empty. Following these rules of Yin and Yang will keep you in balance during your Tai Chi practice.

Bending and Straightening

Bending is Yin, while straightening is Yang. When we bend the arms, legs, and spine we are storing energy; when we straighten them, we release the stored energy. The Tai Chi Classics say, "Storing energy is like bending a bow; releasing energy is like shooting an arrow." For this reason, the arms, legs, and spine are called the Three Bows in Tai Chi. If you want to shoot the arrow a long distance, you must first bend the bow.

Beginners often neglect to bend the knees enough when shifting forward and back. This is why their movements lack power. Too much bending, however, can lead to collapse of one's structure, so it is important to bend neither too little nor too much.

Similarly, straightening the arms or legs too much can also lead to stiffness and overextending. The joints are often referred to in Chi Kung as "the energy gates of the body." Thus, whenever you straighten the arms and legs, you should never lock the knees and elbows; instead you should always keep a slight flexion in these joints to keep the energy gates open. This allows the Chi and blood to flow smoothly through the limbs without the obstruction you create when you lock the joints and inadvertently close the gates.

Up and Down, Advancing and Retreating, Left and Right

The Tai Chi Classics say, "If there is up, there is down; if there is retreating, there is advancing; if there is left, there is right. If your intention is to move up, you should at the same time contain the idea of downward." Up and down are two sides of the same coin, and the same is true of advancing and retreating, left and right. This becomes especially important in Tai Chi martial arts applications and strategy. When moving forward, you should always be ready to instantly retreat if necessary. Similarly, when retreating, you should remain watchful for the opportunity to advance. If you concentrate exclusively on advancing without keeping some mindfulness of retreating, you can easily be led into a trap, and your mind will be unable to shift quickly enough to escape because your mind is too Yang and you have not maintained the seed of Yin in your intent.

If you want to lead your opponent upward, it is good strategy to first apply a slight downward force. Your opponent will tend to try to defend against the false downward attack by moving upward; then you can lead his inten-

Retracting is Yin; Advancing is Yang.

tion, borrow his energy and combine it with yours in your upward attack and effortlessly uproot him.

The same principle holds true with left and right. If you want to attack your opponent's right side, create a diversion by applying a slight force on his left side. If his attention then goes to his left, he may leave his right side undefended, making it easy to attack.

Soft and Hard

The Tai Chi Classics say, "From the greatest softness comes the greatest hardness." Tai Chi Chi Kung is sometimes called a soft style martial art. This is because most martial arts emphasize strength and speed, whereas Tai Chi emphasizes a balance between soft and hard. Still, it is wrong to characterize Tai Chi merely as a soft style, because the name Tai Chi means Yin and Yang, both soft and hard. Some Tai Chi students mistakenly cultivate the soft to the exclusion of the hard, ending up with what is disparagingly referred to by the true masters as "tofu Tai Chi."

While most people can easily understand the power of hardness in the martial arts, the power of softness and yielding seems contradictory and confusing. The strength of Tai Chi is compared to refined spring steel. Spring steel is flexible yet strong, yielding yet powerful. To refine iron ore into spring steel, ore must be melted to a soft molten liquid state many times until all the impurities are removed. Similarly, in Tai Chi training one must first learn to relax and become flexible in every joint until all unnecessary tension and stiffness are refined out of one's movements. As a result one becomes strong yet supple, soft on the outside yet firm on the inside, like steel wrapped in cotton. This is true power, a balance of Yin and Yang.

The principle of balancing softness and hardness is also applied when dealing with an opponent. We meet the opponent's Yang force with Yin and attack their Yin place with Yang. In Tai Chi we never meet the opponent's Yang attack head-on. Instead of facing the brunt of an opponent's Yang force, we yield to it in a soft Yin way. Because Yang always contains Yin, we must at the same time scout out where the opponent is soft and Yin (weak and unguarded) and apply our Yang hard force to that area. We do not waste our Yang force trying to confront our opponent's Yang directly. Instead, we conserve our Yang energy and wait to apply it where it will require the least amount of effort to gain maximum advantage.

Defense and Attack

Many martial arts styles separate defensive and offensive movements into two separate steps. First they block, then they strike. In Tai Chi Chi Kung, Yin and Yang, defense and offense, are integrated into every single movement. Defense and offense usually occur simultaneously in Tai Chi. While one hand is yielding, the other hand is striking; when the upper body is yielding, the lower body is attacking.

Yin/Yang Tendon: Tree Exercise

To better experience and distinguish the Yin and Yang force, the Tree Exercise provides a means of emphasizing these subtle energy differences.

1. Find a healthy, beautiful green tree, and begin by directing the Ward Off movement toward the tree, with your right leg and right arm in front.

2. Start with a very slow in-breath. Feel the Earth force pulling the sacrum down. The Heavenly force produces a corresponding counterpull up. Begin to push the right

leg into the earth, moving the structure backward without moving the hands.

The feet remain in place. Straighten the right wrist so the palm no longer faces the body but now faces the left side. Position the left hand so the palm faces up.

Yin-Yang exercise with tree.

3. Sink back deeply into the left foot and feel the weight of the entire body being supported by the foot, sole, heel, and hip. As you sink back, bring the left hand under the right hand and pass it along the underside of the right arm until it is just under the right elbow. This is known as Protecting the Elbow.

This is the Yin portion of the exercise, and so during the sinking, the energy is drawn in through the fingertips, through the tendons of the arms, and down through the rest of the tendons of the structure. Focus the attention on drawing the energy from the tree as a rich supply of healthy energy.

Take care to keep the chest sunk and the arms rounded. Don't allow the right arm to collapse so that it comes closer to the body. In sinking back, often the pelvis gets twisted sideways in the direction of the left leg. A combination of factors causes this to happen: one is rigidity in the muscles and ligaments connecting the hip bone to the spine and legs; second is excessive sinking down so the central line of gravity passes beyond the sole of the left foot. By twisting sideways, the center of gravity is somewhat restored, but the alignment with the spine is lost. This problem is particularly common among women. Exercises to loosen the hips should be regularly practiced, along with lower abdominal breathing.

4. When fully sunk, you now begin the Yang phase. This time, the hands do not move at all. Maintaining your position, you initiate this phase by slowly exhaling and pressing the left leg into the ground. This creates a force from the opened groin onto the tendons of the legs, which now receive the rebounding Earth force. Based on the correctness of your structure, the Earth energy travels up the tendons of the body, past the hip to the C-7 vertebra, through the tendons of the right arm and out the fingers toward the tree. Here the tree absorbs the Yang energy you are generating.

Once you have sensitized yourself to the subtle exchanges of Yin and Yang energies with the tree, you can continue this exercise without a loss of energy, because you are sharing the Yin and Yang phases of give and take with the tree.

Keep the breath inhalations and exhalations corresponding to the Yin and Yang motions of the exercise for consistency. All motions should be as slow and smooth as possible for optimum results.

YIN AND YANG/ INNER SMILE FORM

From the previous illustrations and exercises, you will be able to understand and apply the principles of Yin and Yang throughout your practice of Tai Chi Chi Kung. We have provided a step-by-step explanation of the Introductory Movements to help you get the idea.

In the subsequent Core Movements, apply the principles of Yin and Yang as described earlier in this chapter.

Introductory Movements

Wu Chi Stance

Smile

The Inner Smile plays a particularly important role in the Wu Chi stance. Wu Chi means Supreme Nothingness or Pure Openness. When we begin by smiling to the throat center or parathyroid, this opens up our ability to express. To participate in the interaction of Yin and Yang, the emphasis is placed on the ability to change with grace and smoothness. When the throat center is open, one has a willingness to change.

Smiling in Tai Chi practice expresses a happy connectedness with the universe. Smiling also helps eliminate tension (the kind you get when you have a lump in your throat from anxiety).

Next, smile to the muscles. This helps correct any excess tension caused by unnecessary structural reliance on the muscles and aids in transferring more of the load-bearing effort to the tendons and bones. If the muscles are separated from the bones, then the Chi can flow.

Finally, smile to the tendons and bones to properly prepare the body for motion. This is particularly important later on for the proper execution of the Changing the Tendons Form and the Bone Breathing Form.

Breathing and Drawing Energy

The breath helps direct the phases of the motion. *Inhalation is Yin (gathering the force), while exhalation is Yang (expressing and releasing*

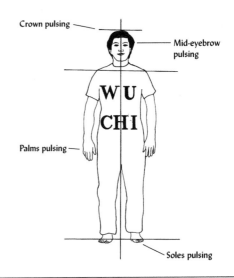

the force). It also acts as a measure of the Lesser, Greater, and Greatest partitioning of the Yin and Yang cycles. During the course of the entire form, it is essential that the practitioner never run out of breath or be caused to suck in air quickly to continue. The breath should be as smooth, slow, and even as the motions. It is said that if you control the breath, then you control your life.

Paying careful attention to the pulsing in the palms, mid-eyebrow, crown, and soles is useful in coordinating the breath and the Chi flow with the motions. You should also pay attention to the pulsing in the joints when in the Wu Chi stance, especially in the spinal joints.

Opening Tai Chi

Preparation

The weight transfer begins by sinking down onto the right leg. In this way, lighter weight is Yin and heavier weight is Yang. Also, left is Yin and right is Yang, as it is naturally in the body. These right and left roles are reversed during the transitions into the various directions. Again, the back must maintain the connection between Earth (Yin) and Heaven (Yang).

Step Out

Stepping out leads to an equal distribution of weight between the legs, balance between Yin and Yang. This phase emphasizes Wu Chi, the nothingness that exists beyond the Yin and Yang; it is the subtle equipoise from which Yin and Yang later emerge as Tai Chi.

Raising the Arms

The fingertips, facing downward, connect with the Earth energy and draw in the cool, healing, blue electric-like current during the Yin phase of Raising the Arms. This is followed by the Yang phase, where the arms move outward and lightly float up toward heaven. When the wrists reach shoulder height, a transition to Yin begins as the arms bend and contract inward in preparation for the Two Hand Push.

Raising the arms (Yin).

Two Hand Push

The rippling action of the Two Hand Push is the Yang action of guiding the Earth energy up through the body out in the direction of the push. Iron Shirt Chi Kung II particularly emphasizes this skill; the tendons conduct the energy flow in synchronization with the Chi pulsing. Start the motion at the nine points of

Preparation

Step out: Balance of Yin and Yang.

The Two Hand Push exhale – Yang.

the feet, which you press into the earth, creating a wave that travels up through the knees, groin, and hip to the sacrum. Relax the psoas and tuck the sacrum at just the right moment to propel the wave up your spine to C-7, where you increase the wave by tucking your chin and direct it out the shoulders, elbows, and wrists to the palms. Completely direct the motion by the tendon power of your whole body; the hands never move independently.

Lowering the Arms

The Yin phase involves gently retracting the tendons and bringing the wrists back in toward the body, still at shoulder level. Then, with arms relaxed and passive, exhale and let the Earth force of gravity draw the arms down to the level of the hips.

Raise the arms and inhale - Yin   Bring hands down and exhale - Yang

SUMMARY

As you can see, there are many aspects to the expression of Yin and Yang in the Tai Chi Chi Kung form. In the Tao Te Ching it is said, "The journey of a thousand miles begins with a single step." The best way to learn is to focus on one of the principles at a time. Choose one aspect of Yin and Yang as described earlier in this chapter, and make it the focus of your practice until you have mastered and integrated it within all the movements of your Tai Chi Chi Kung form. Then move on to the next one. In this way, step by step, you will soon master all the various elements of Yin and Yang.

8

Rooting and Grounding: Connecting with the Earth

What is Rooting?

One dictionary definition of root is "the source or origin of an action, quality, etc." This definition echoes the Tai Chi Classics: "Each movement is rooted in the feet, developed in the legs, directed by the waist, and expressed through the fingers and hands."

The physical process of rooting involves aligning the skeletal structure with gravity. The resulting connection with the earth allows a free exchange of force down through the skeletal structure into the earth and back up from the earth through the structure.

Rooting and Self-Defense

Rooting is essential to all aspects of Tai Chi Chi Kung: defending, neutralizing, and attacking. In terms of defense, the ability to redirect any horizontal force vertically into the ground makes a rooted person nearly impossible to push over. The effect is similar to driving a stake into the ground. The more pressure applied, the more firmly the stake is driven into the ground.

Neutralizing or deflecting can be accomplished from a rooted position without the risk of being knocked off balance. The power for all offense, such as Ward Off, Push, and Press, comes from the flexion and subsequent extension of the legs.

Developing the Leg Force

The leg muscles are the strongest muscles in the body. In this society, they have become little more than means to convey the head and arms from place to place; however, they play a very large role in Tai Chi Chi Kung. Ninety percent of the force in Tai Chi Chi Kung comes from the legs. This force cannot be used unless it is supported by a stable base in the feet. If the feet are not properly positioned, the body becomes like a tree with half its roots damaged. Such a tree would have difficulty drawing enough nutrients up from the soil. Additionally, it would be susceptible to being blown over in a wind storm.

Wu Wei and Rooting

A goal of Tai Chi Chi Kung is to produce the maximum force with the minimum effort. The Taoists call this principle Wu-Wei or effortlessness. Hence, the emphasis in Tai Chi Chi Kung is on relaxing the muscles and shifting the load-bearing effort to the skeletal structure and tendons instead. Excess tension drains energy, whereas correct Tai Chi Chi Kung practice generates energy and increases Chi. This surplus of Chi then becomes available for healing or spiritual work.

The Importance of Connecting to the Yin Earth Energy Through Rooting

Higher levels of spiritual work involve drawing in large amounts of Heavenly Yang energy. People who do not have an effective way of grounding that energy and balancing it with the Yin Earth energy may resort to drugs, sex, alcohol, and overeating to get the Yin they need. Many of the well-known Tai Chi masters of the past fell victim to these vices in a misguided attempt to balance their excess Yang. These means have negative health consequences. In the Healing Tao, because of the emphasis on drawing in the pure Yin energies of the earth while rooting, one can do higher-level meditations without abusing drugs, sex, alcohol, or food.

In my book *Iron Shirt Chi Kung I*, I have given point-by-point descriptions of how to connect the whole structure together. Readers are referred to that book for further references on aligning the structure.

The Nine Points of the Feet

The skeletal structure is designed to distribute the weight of the body evenly over the nine points of the foot. If you were to put ink on the soles of your feet and step on a piece of paper, the nine points would be revealed in the print: the heel point, the outer edge of the foot, the small ball, the large ball, and the five toes. Distributing the bodily weight evenly among these points provides a stable foundation for the rest of the structure.

By contrast, uneven weight distribution results in instability, unnecessary tension, and loss of power. One indication of uneven weight distribution is the wear pattern on shoes. Shoes that have been worn for a while develop uneven wear patterns if one part of the foot is habitually stressed more than other parts.

Bubbling Spring Point

The importance of the connection the feet make with the ground is recognized in sports. Shoes designed for specific sports are proliferating. Now, every sport has its own shoe. Each shoe manufacturer attempts to develop a model that will give its wearers a competitive edge. Shoes for sports performed on grass even have cleats to help players root to the ground. In Tai Chi Chi Kung, a similar result is obtained by applying knowledge of anatomy.

Not using all nine points of the foot is like leaning back in a chair so that only two of the chair's legs are touching the ground: the resulting position is unstable. Attention that could have been focused on the task at hand, had one been sitting stably on all four legs of the chair, must be diverted to maintain balance. It also requires unnecessary muscular effort.

Not standing on all nine points of the feet is also like running a galley ship where only half the slaves row. Only half the available manpower goes into moving the boat. In addition, the slaves who do not row are gradually weakened by inactivity; hence, an already reduced source of power continues to diminish. Tai Chi practitioners who break their root significantly decrease their power by rolling off their base of support so that either the heel, toes, or outside edge of the foot comes off the floor.

ROOTING EXERCISES
Tai Chi Walking

During the day, it is good to be aware of your feet as you walk. The following exercise, Tai Chi Walking, will help you be more conscious of the feet in walking.

1. Step forward, touching the heel down very lightly before shifting weight onto it.

2. Slowly roll onto the outer edge of the foot, then onto the small ball under the little toe and the large ball under the big toe. Then roll onto the toes, the big toe, second, third, fourth, and little toes. Feel your weight evenly distributed.

3. Shift your weight back to your rear foot. As you do, be mindful of keeping the nine points of your rear foot flat on the ground; be sure not to lift your heel.

4. Lift the toes, small ball, large ball, and outer edge of the front foot off the ground, and then rotate your front foot out 45 degrees.

5. Roll onto the front foot; shift all your weight to that foot. Balance and step out straight with the free foot, touching your heel down first, very lightly.

6. Repeat steps 2-5 up to 20 times to really feel the nine points deeply.

With each step, feel the sense of the nine points touching the ground. When you press the nine points to the ground and relax, you activate the Earth force. When you are aware of the bones and the nine points and relax, you will gradually feel the Earth force transform from the ground up into the bone structure.

The relaxation phase is very important. Rest and feel the energy. The more you relax, the more easily you will feel the force; the more you tense, the more the muscles clamp into the bone and the harder it is for Chi to flow. When you relax, Chi flows very easily through the bones, the fascial layers, and the muscles. When you press the bones, the bones will produce more Chi.

This precise way of stepping is in contrast to the way most people walk, which is a slightly refined version of the way a toddler walks. To begin a step, the torso is inclined forward. One avoids falling by catching the weight on a foot that is rapidly thrown out in front. With each step, the entire structure is jarred. Among the organs, the kidneys are particularly adversely affected. Unless one makes a conscious effort at retraining, walking continues to be a process of falling and catching oneself. Contrast this to the calculated steps of a cat stalking, which is what we seek to emulate in Tai Chi Chi Kung.

Spiraling to Weld the Structure Together

Spiraling links the structure of the legs together in a very powerful way. The bones of the hip are connected to the femur (the thigh bone), which connects at the knee to the two bones in the calf (the tibia and fibula), which then join the foot at the ankle.

1. Begin standing with the feet shoulder-width apart, knees slightly bent. Tuck the sacrum and sink the coccyx until the feet press more firmly into the ground. Essentially, this movement directs the Tan Tien Chi down through the legs into the feet and into the earth. If the upper body is vertically aligned, all its weight stacks on the hips.

Press feet firmly against the ground.

2. Smile to the groin area. Let it loosen until it feels like an empty bucket.
3. Open the groin, pressing out with the upper thigh. This movement initiates a spiral down the legs: counterclockwise down the left leg, and clockwise down the right leg.
4. Amplify the spiral at the knees by gently pressing them down and out.
5. The spiral continues down through the calf to the ankles and to the feet. The feet spiral out.
6. The force is transferred evenly to all nine parts of the feet: the heel, the outside of the foot, the small ball under the little toe, the large ball under the big toe, and the five toes.

Knee Practice

1. Assume the Bow and Arrow stance, with the left foot back, the right foot forward.

Twist the knee gently outward and feel the force screwing into the ground.

2. Feel the nine points, and feel both feet touching the ground. You can have your weight supported by both feet 50-50, or front leg 70 percent, back leg 30 percent.
3. Now be aware of the knee. Press the feet to the ground, and slightly twist the left knee counterclockwise and the right knee clockwise. Relax and feel the Chi flow up from the earth through the feet, up to the knee, and up to the hip. Repeat a few times. Then change legs.
4. When you change legs, with the left leg in front, you will twist in the reverse direction.

Knee Practice with a Partner

1. While standing with the knee twisted, have a partner push on the outside of the knee. Have the partner start pushing with one hand, and increase to two hands.

rear leg is analogous to bending the bow. Feel that you are gathering your strength like a horse preparing to jump a stream or fence.

Initiate the movement forward by sinking the groin and connecting the coccyx to the feet. Spiral both feet. If the right foot is forward, the spiral for that leg is in a clockwise direction. If the left foot is forward, the spiral for that leg is in the counterclockwise direction. As you move forward, continue spiraling. Stopping spiraling is like leaking air out of a tire; you lose all the force you have generated. When the advance is completed, the hips should be square to the front.

2. To emphasize how much the twisting of the knee increases the power, repeat the exercise. This time try not to twist the knee. Press the feet into the ground as hard as you can, and have your partner push you on the knee. Observe the difference.

Spiraling multiplies the force of an advance.

In Tai Chi Chi Kung, spiraling in the legs is emphasized throughout the advancing (shifting forward) movements such as Ward Off, Press, and Push. The feet need to be properly positioned. How far forward the front foot is placed relative to the back foot is determined by how far you can step forward with all the weight still balanced on the rear leg. Attempts to exceed this length in stepping result in instability. The two feet should be shoulder-width apart. The rear foot should be at a 45-degree angle to the front foot.

To begin the advance, all the weight should be on the rear leg. The legs are considered one of the three bows of the body. Sinking into the

THE ROOTING FORM

In the Rooting Form, you incorporate all the principles and skills you have learned through the rooting exercises. To evaluate your rooting skills, have a partner test your structure in each of the postures illustrated in this section.

Opening Movements

Wu Chi Stance

The Wu Chi stance is particularly important for setting the rootedness of the Tai Chi practice. The "nothingness" can be achieved only with appropriate connectedness to both Heaven and Earth, which implies rooting. The following checks should therefore be made to determine the effectiveness of the Wu Chi stance for rooting:

- the nine points of the foot connect to the ground properly
- the feet are relaxed and open
- the muscles are relaxed and the tendons activated
- the knees are slightly bent, opening the energy gates to the Earth force
- the groin (kua or hip joint) is open
- the pelvis is square to the North
- the psoas muscles are relaxed
- the sacrum and coccyx are aligned to the ground
- the spine is erect
- the chin is gently tucked.

In addition, and just as important to a correctly rooted structure, the mind is relaxed. Smile to all the joints that affect the rooting: ankles, knees, and hips. This mental rootedness is required for the energy from the earth to move freely into the stance. Rootedness can be verified each time by sensing a cool and comfortable connection with the blue Earth energy.

Once you are in this stance, have a partner place one hand on your shoulder and the other on your hip and push you. If your structure and rooting are correct, the force will transfer to the ground.

Opening Tai Chi

The Opening Tai Chi movement involves sinking the weight into the Earth force. This provides an increased connectedness with the rooting force of gravity. The mind should relate the two as the body sinks by sensing the increased earth pull, as if the weight is actually being brought by the earth toward itself. The transition of weight from one leg to the other allows the practitioner the opportunity to become sensitized to rooting on the left and right legs.

Core Movements: Left Hand Form

Grasp The Bird's Tail

First Ward Off: Holding the Chi Ball

When you shift weight to the left leg and extend the right leg forward, the distance of the right leg plays an important role in the rootedness of the form. You should place your forward leg with a completely opened groin, relaxed to full extension and with the heel touching the ground comfortably. Picture this movement as a drafting compass, with the leg acting as a pencil. Once the groin is opened, and the appropriate angle of sweep has been traversed, there is virtually only one correct location to place the heel. If done properly, this ensures that the next Yang actions will have a properly rooted stance, which efficiently draws energy from the earth. Without a properly selected position, the stance will be either too wide or too short, leading to poor rooting.

Correct structure and rooting will transfer energy to the ground.

Rooting in first Ward Off.

Second Ward Off: Holding the Chi Ball

In the Yang portions of the Ward Off, rooting action is most important. The nine points must have the correct contact on both the front and back foot The ankles must be torqued opposite to the knees to provide the necessary activation on the tendons of the ankles. The left knee is lightly twisted counterclockwise and the right knee is lightly twisted clockwise; both are torqued in an outward direction with the force generated by opening of the groin. With a tucked sacrum and properly squared hips, the lower structure is then properly rooted and aligned and can act as a conduit of Earth energy for the upper body to allow the wave motion to direct the Yang action.

It is very important to thrust your pinky finger inward, your thumb out, and to feel this torque in your wrist and elbow. You must also round the scapulae to connect the arms to the spine.

Mental sensitization to the spiraling action of the energy up the legs assists in proper rooting to the earth. Also, it is critical that the action begin as an impulse with the soles of the feet pressing into the ground, followed by an immediate push off of the back heel. This creates the impulse that rebounds the Earth energy up the tendons of the body. While both feet are used for this purpose, the back foot serves as the primary power source, with the right foot acting as the supportive secondary source.

Rollback

During the Rollback, the feet are stationary and firmly connected to the Earth. Feel the energy spiral up through the knees, with the hips and waist carrying the upper body along. This twists the tendons and creates a spiraling

of the Earth energy. Use the mind to root during this turn so you feel the energy connecting to the earth through the spirals around the legs.

Two Hand Press

The Two Hand Press uses the same rooting techniques that were described for the Second Ward Off; only the arm action is different.

Two Hand Push

The Two Hand Push also uses the same rooting techniques that were described for the Second Ward Off. Only the arm action is different to implement the push.

Single Whip: South

The First Twist

Keep the back leg rooted during the torquing action of the pivot. Use your mind to root during the pivot so you feel the energy connecting to the Earth through the spirals around the back leg. The back knee leads the way, with the foot locked into the ground as the energy is drawn up the leg in preparation for the strike.

Making the Beak (Second Twist)

When you transfer your weight to the right leg, connect down through the nine points and lock into the earth, as the same action occurs in reverse.

Releasing the Beak (Third Twist)

Here you release the torqued force gathered in the right leg. The left foot disconnects when it is raised on the balls of the foot, such that the full storage of power is in the right leg just prior to the strike. Feel the spiral from the foot through the leg. Open the right groin and feel the spiral continue up through the trunk, through the shoulder, and out into the right arm. The right foot should remain locked with the nine points rooted into the earth, so the energy is effectively released with the beak.

Twist wrist and elbow like a screw.   Shoulder sinks.

Elbow sinks.

Reaching Up to Heaven

Once again, the distance the leg sweeps out is particularly important in the rooting of the Yang actions that follow. The leg should be straight, with the groin open and the heel of the foot placed lightly on the ground in a fully extended position. When the foot cuts down and the weight is shifted between the left and right legs, pay special attention to mentally

rooting into the ground as the Yang action reaches up to Heaven.

Single Hand Push

The Single Hand Push, like the previous Yang actions, has the same rooting as was described for the Second Ward Off. The only difference is the action of the arms to implement the push.

Shoulder sinks.

Elbow sinks.

Transition Movements
Protecting the Chest

The Protecting the Chest action, like the Single Hand Push, has the same rooting as was described for the Second Ward Off. The only difference is the action of the arms to implement the protection of the chest.

Holding the Baby

The nine points of the feet are locked into the earth during this motion to maintain the rootedness that was set up by the single hand push to the North.

Closing Movements
Cross Hands

It is particularly important when stepping backward that you step in a graceful, balanced and rooted way, like a cat walking. The sinking, followed by the slow extension of the knees, is all performed while keeping in mind your firm connection to the earth.

Hun Yuan Stance

The Hun Yuan stance is completed with rootedness in exactly the same manner as at the start of the form.

9

Transferring Chi Through the Body

MOVING THE FORCE THROUGH THE SPINE

The goal of connecting to the Earth force by rooting is to bring the energy from the feet all the way up to the hands. Although the feet and legs are the structural foundation, having structure in the lower body alone is not enough in itself. The force that we have developed in the legs through rooting practice tends to get jammed in the curved parts of the spine.

The remedy is to straighten the curves in the three sections of the back: lumbar, thoracic, and cervical. Force will then transfer smoothly through a straight spine. A straight spine is like a straight stick. Pushing on this stick will drive it into the ground. The harder the push, the deeper the stick will go. On the other hand, pushing hard on a stick with a bend or kink in it will break the stick.

We emphasize working from the coccyx and sacrum up the spine to straighten it. The coccyx and sacrum form the lowest part of the spine. When the sacrum sticks out, all the lumbar vertebrae become closed. When the sacrum is dropped and aligned with the foot, these lumbar vertebrae are opened. The sacrum is

aligned to open the lumbar vertebrae, which begins the process of lengthening the spine.

The thoracic vertebra are also curved. Pushing out at the T-11 vertebra serves to straighten this curve and further elongate the spine. The T-5/T-6 vertebrae are linked to the rest of the spine by sinking the chest. The curve of the cervical spine is straightened by pushing back at C7 and the Jade Pillow. The spinal processes are then opened and loosened. Having been transferred up thus far, the force is then transmitted through the scapulae out through the arms to the hands.

ALIGNING THE SPINE
Practice: Sacrum

1. Have your partner press a fist against your sacrum.
2. Move the sacrum forward and back until you feel you are aligned. Then put your hands on the lumbar region.
3. Tilt the sacrum under (in). Then push it back, but keep the lumbar region open. Pushing out too far will close the lumbar region.

    The lumbar region should feel expanded like a balloon. When the sacrum is properly aligned, you will feel the feet pressed more firmly into the ground as the force of the push is connected to them.

We learn to place the structure in such an aligned way that a great force applied to the structure can travel to the ground without tilting a person off balance.

T-11

The 11th thoracic vertebra (T-11) is also called the adrenal center due to its close proximity to the adrenal glands. A good way to find T-11 is to find the point midway between the bottom of the sternum and the navel in the front; we call this the solar plexus point. Draw your finger around to the point on the spine opposite the solar plexus; this is T-11. If you put your hand on this point and lean forward, you'll notice that it protrudes more than any of the surrounding vertebrae.

Have your partner bring a fist up to T-11. Push out so the curve in the lower back is straightened, becoming full and expanded. Push back strongly against your partner's fist as if you were going to push him or her over.

Starting the push at T-11.

Again, feel the pressure in the feet as the force is transferred to the ground.

Inhaling into T-11.

C-7

C-7 is the seventh and lowest cervical vertebra. The Chinese name for C-7, Ta Chui, means "big vertebra." It is the big bone at the base of the neck.

Have your partner push on C-7 with a palm. The best way to feel the C-7 force is to simulate stopping suddenly in your car: push the feet into the ground, straighten the legs, tightly grab the steering wheel, lock the elbows, and push the chin in and the C-7 and Jade Pillow out. Ordinarily we don't exercise the neck like this, but with practice you will automatically have this response; it could save your neck in a traumatic situation.

Pull the chin in.

Pushing at C-7 and T-2 with palm.

Jade Pillow

Have your partner put the palm of his/her hand on the Jade Pillow. Your partner should be careful not to apply too much pressure at this point; have your partner give only the lightest resistance. Push back, generating Jade Pillow force by pulling in the chin while simultaneously raising the crown.

Pushing at the base of the skull.

Practice Spinal Alignment by Yourself: Standing

1. If you don't have a partner, you can use a wall. Stand with the feet parallel and shoulder-width apart, the spine touching the wall. Relax the sacrum.

2. Press the feet to the ground. Twist the knee, square the hip, and press the sacrum to the wall. Hold for a while and relax. Feel the Chi flow up to the sacrum.
3. Press T-11 against the wall. Hold for a while and relax. Feel the Chi flow up to the sacrum and T-11.

Wall

Press the Tan Tien Chi down and back.

4. Sink the sternum, push the chin in, round the scapulae, and bring C-7 near the wall. Hold for a while and relax. Feel the Chi flow up through the sacrum, T-11, and C-7.

Spinal Alignment Floor Exercise

1. Lie down on the floor. Feel the spine touching the floor. Draw both knees up and feel the feet touching the ground.
2. Press the feet to the ground, and feel the sacrum, the spine, and the head moved by the feet. Repeat a few times, and observe how the feet can move the whole body. Relax and feel the Chi flow.
3. Now, press the feet to the ground. Press the sacrum and T-11 to the ground. Feel the sacrum and T-11 touching the ground, and feel the alignment. Extend both arms, sink the chest, push the chin in, and feel the C-7 point touch the ground. Relax and feel the Chi flow.

Press the Tan Tien Chi to the back.

1. Press the foot. 2. Push the sacrum to the ground.
3. Push T-11 to the ground. 4. Press C-7 to the ground.
5. The head will automatically extend up because of the lengthening of the spine. 6. The arms, extended by rounding the scapulae, connect to the force developed in the spine.

Sinking the Chest Practice

1. Have your partner put her hand on the center of your chest, on the sternum.

Sinking the chest.

2. Stick the chest out in an exaggerated fashion.
3. Have your partner gradually push on the sternum. Don't let her move you back. Exhale, drop the chest, and round the scapula and back. Transfer the force down the front of the body to the ground. Feel the nine points of the feet being pressed more firmly into the ground.

Sink the chest and align the skeletal structure of the spine, pelvis, and legs to transfer the force to the ground.

Sinking the chest is an important part of rooting. This is very useful when someone pushes you. He may expect you to be moved back, but if you can root, you can come back with another technique right away.

Sinking the sternum forces breath into the back of the lungs, and energy is automatically directed down into the abdomen; you breathe more into the lower Tan Tien, draining all the tension down.

The spinal cord is like a drive train, the axle of a car. The hips are like the back-wheel drive. The scapula are like the front-wheel drive. When you put them together, you have four-wheel drive. Integrate them, and you can transfer force. This is called locking the structure. When the structure is right, you can take a lot of force in and discharge an equivalent amount of force.

The hips transfer weight to the ground. Also, the Earth force comes up through the feet and legs to the hip, through the spine, and the scapulae transfer it out to the hands. Alternatively, force can be transferred from the hands down through the structure to the feet and into the earth.

THE SCAPULA AND ELBOW CONNECTIONS

The Scapula Connection

What we call the shoulder is actually made up of three bones: the scapula (shoulder blade), the clavicle (collarbone), and the humerus (upper arm bone). The shoulder is

The arm connects with the scapula

The sternum moves in and the rib cage sinks in

Correctly rounded scapulae

The arm is not connected with the scapula

The sternum remains out and the rib cage remains out

Incorrect rounding of the scapulae.

All the tendons, muscles, and ligaments are fully extended from the spine across the back, through the shoulders and arms, to the fingertips.

designed for free range of movement, so the only place the shoulder is actually attached bone to bone to the rib cage is at the point where the clavicle attaches to the top of the sternum (breastbone). The scapulae themselves float over the rib cage in the back, attached only to the clavicle and humerus. This gives the advantage of flexibility and increases the range of motion of the shoulder. The disadvantage is that because this joint structure is so flexible and free, it can easily become a place where we break or lose structural integrity.

In Tai Chi, we need to be able to direct and connect the force we have generated in the legs and hips up the spine and out into the arms. To accomplish this, we round the scapulae. Rounding the scapulae means to sink the chest, pull the chin in, pull the C-7 and Jade Pillow back, and separate the two scapulae as far apart as they can go. When you do this, the shoulder moves forward, the scapulae press firmly against the rib cage, joining strongly or "sticking" to the rib cage and no longer protruding back. From the top view, the upper back appears rounded, and the scapulae will feel powerful. Many animals naturally use scapulae power. If you watch a tiger move, it walks with scapulae power. When it claws, its incredible energy comes from moving the scapulae.

Practice the Scapulae Connection by Yourself: On the Floor

Exercise 1

1. Lie down on the back on the floor. Raise the knees up. Rest the feet on the floor, about shoulder-width apart.

2. Raise the arms until they are perpendicular to the floor, pointing toward the ceiling. Keep the arms straight, and for this exercise, keep the elbows locked (in the actual Tai Chi form, you would never lock the elbows).

3. Feel the scapulae touching the floor.

4. Keeping the arms straight, lift the scapulae as far from the floor as possible. Notice

how this moves the hands several inches closer to the ceiling.

Tan Tien Chi

Press the Chi Ball to the floor.

5. Lower the scapulae to touch the floor, still keeping the arms straight and pointed up.

6. Repeat steps 4 and 5 several times. Experiment with doing it both slowly and quickly, but without excess strain.

7. When finished, lower the arms down to the sides. Rest, and feel the Chi flow.

Exercise 2

1. Lie down on the back on the floor. Raise the knees up. Rest the feet on the floor, about shoulder-width apart.

2. Raise the arms until they are perpendicular to the floor, pointing toward the ceiling. Keep the arms straight, and for this exercise, keep the elbows locked (in the actual Tai Chi form, you would never lock the elbows).

3. Feel the scapulae touching the floor.

4. Tuck in the sacrum. Feel the feet connect to the ground.

5. Feel the connection from the feet up through the legs through the sacrum, like

a wave of force. Feel the connection/wave on up to T-11 and C-7. Pull in the chin.

6. Sink the sternum down as you raise the scapulae, as you did in Exercise 1. Feel the connection from the feet up through the hands.

7. Lower the scapulae, relax the sacrum, and relax everything else, but keep the arms up.

8. Repeat steps 4-7 several times. Feel the wavelike force each time, from the sacrum to the feet, and on up to the arms.

9. Bring the arms back to the sides. Rest, and feel the Chi flow.

The Elbow Connection

Once you are able to connect the shoulder to the spine, if you also have all the aforementioned points in line, you can now move the energy from the ground up and out into the arm. However, the force will never reach the hand unless you have the elbow connection.

In the Tai Chi Classics, the old masters instruct us to sink the shoulders and elbows. This means that in most postures and movements, the elbows should point toward the ground.

To get a feeling for this, have someone hold your arm up by the wrist. Let the arm relax completely. In this relaxed position, the elbows will automatically point toward the ground. You are not using any extra energy to hold the elbow out in a strained posture, so you can efficiently direct all the force out into the hands.

Another important structural point is that you want to have the elbows fairly straight in a discharging-energy posture, yet not locked. At a minimum, the forearm and upper arm should always be at an angle greater than 90 degrees. At a maximum, the elbow can be at nearly 180 degrees, but the elbow joint should still never be locked stiff.

Practice: Transferring the Force from the Ground

1. Start from a back-weighted position with the arms held in the Push position. Inhale as you shift back.

Sink the shoulders

Sink the elbows

Inhale and draw in the Chi.

2. Exhale and advance until you are nearly to the end of the push.

3. As the knee comes over the foot, straighten the spine from the bottom to the top.

Tan Tien Chi

1. Press the Tan Tien Chi to the ground, feel the big toes lightly turn outward. 2. Gently spiral the knees outward. 3. Tuck in the sacrum. 4. Open the groin by lengthening the psoas muscle. 5. Round the lower back, push T-11 back. 6. Sink the chest and push back at T-5. 7. Round the scapulae. 8. Pull the chin in and raise the crown.

4. Tuck the sacrum; feel the lumbar connect with the earth.

5. Push out T-11.

6. Sink the chest. Push out at T-5/T-6.

7. Round the scapulae. Extend the ligaments at the elbow, wrist, and fingers.

8. Pull in the chin and raise the crown.

9. Feel the energy ripple through and then release.

10. Do this in a very relaxed way, not forcefully. Practice this 30-40 times a day. Practice until the movement becomes natural.

A Principle of Pushing: The Chin Direction

The direction of the chin depends on the direction you are pushing. If you push to the front, straighten the cervical spine and raise the crown as described. If you push to the left, you turn the chin slightly to the right, just a little bit, not too much. When you push to the right, push the chin a little to the left. When you push the force down, the chin is a little more up. This is a very subtle internal movement.

SUMMARY

Now you can apply the principles you have learned through these exercises in each of the Tai Chi Chi Kung movements. Make sure the whole body is connected from the beginning of the form to the end. There is not a single movement where the hands and arms move without the initiation of the rest of the body. You will have mastered this phase when, with every movement, "The power is rooted in the foot, developed in the legs, directed by the hips [and sacrum], clinging to the spine, and expressed through the hands."

10
Activating the Tendons

WHY THE TENDONS?

Tai Chi practitioners aspire to be like "steel wrapped in cotton." This describes a state in which the muscles are relaxed, as soft as cotton. Underneath, the tendons, ligaments, and bones are extremely strong. Mastering the Tendon Activation Form, which involves "Changing the Tendons," is critical to attaining the quality of "steel wrapped in cotton."

Tendons join muscles to bones. Most tendons are composed of dense connective (collagenous) tissue. This silvery-white tissue also forms the ligaments (which attach bones to other bones), deep fasciae (sheets of connective tissue wrapped around muscles to hold them in place), and membrane capsules around the kidneys, heart, testes, liver, and lymph nodes. Connective tissue is extremely strong, yet pliable. The lungs, vocal cords, and ligaments between successive vertebrae are composed of a more elastic connective tissue.

Medical research has recently discovered the load-bearing function of these connective tissues. The tendons and ligaments can actually perform this function much more efficiently than muscles can. Apparently, practical experience in martial arts revealed this fact to the Chinese long ago. Hence, the Chinese emphasize training tendons over building the big bulky muscles that are taken as the sign of physical fitness in the West today.

Maintaining the muscles requires the consumption of large quantities of food, particularly protein. Exercise must be extremely vigorous to increase muscle bulk. This type of exercise would tend to cause one to expend, rather than gain, Chi. Overemphasizing the muscles in training eventually results in restricted mobility. Muscle-bound athletes are notoriously inflexible.

Muscles necessarily deteriorate with age, which puts to waste much of the effort spent in building them. By contrast, if trained, the tendons maintain their strength and flexibility. Furthermore the rubbery quality of the tendons allows them to store power (Jing) when twisted. Maintaining springy, flexible tendons can prevent the stiffness that usually accompanies old age.

Tai Chi Chi Kung uses the structure, coordinated by tendon movement, to achieve tremendous power with very little effort. The effectiveness of using the whole body to push someone is easily demonstrated. If you were to attempt to push someone using just one finger, you would strain much and accomplish little. Incorporate the rest of your hand by bending your wrist, and you find you can exert more pressure with less effort. Add the force of your entire arm, and you increase your power geometrically.

In the Tendon Activation Form, the tendons and ligaments, are used to transmit a wavelike force. The push issues out of the ground and passes through the feet, legs, spine, and arms. The force is multiplied as it passes through the body. With so much force concentrated in so small an area (in this case, one fingertip), real damage can be inflicted.

1. When storing energy prior to discharge, the tendons and ligaments contract, closing the joints.

2. When discharging energy, the tendons and ligaments extend, opening the joints. As the joints open, they fill with Chi, which also serves as a cushion.

Training and strengthening the tendons is traditionally called Changing the Tendons. In the Healing Tao system, the complete practice of Changing the Tendons is taught in Iron Shirt Chi Kung II. Changing the tendons does not mean physically replacing them. Instead, the weak tendons are made strong yet flexible. The entire physical system, especially the joints, is affected by this training. Over time, a weak body is changed into a strong one with an abundant supply of Chi. As the joints open, they become filed with Chi. Chi is led to the marrow and brain to nourish them in a practice called Washing the Marrow, which is taught in Bone Marrow Nei Kung, the third level of Iron Shirt Chi Kung.

Mind-Eye-Heart Style

The Mind-Eye-Heart style is the most powerful approach to Changing the Tendons. According to the ancient adage, "The I (pronounced "ee") leads and the Chi follows. The Chi leads and the body follows." The I is the combination of the mind, senses, heart, and organs together. Throughout the Tai Chi Chi Kung form, the mind-eye-heart is used to lead the Chi and move the body.

The heart controls the tendons. When you still the mind and relax completely, you can feel the blood pumping through the arteries as the heart contracts. The Tendon Activation practice involves pairing the movement of the tendons to the heartbeat.

The expanding movement of the tendons can be intensified by using the mind and eyes. The potential of using mind power to affect bodily processes has recently received attention. Patients who could not be helped by mainstream medical therapies have cured themselves through visualizing diseased parts of their bodies as healthy. Meditations in the Healing Tao system provide experience in moving energy in a seated posture. This experience makes transfer to a moving context, such as Tai Chi Chi Kung, much easier.

The eyes help direct and focus the attention. In addition, the eyes are connected to numerous tendons. By stretching the tendons around the eyes, the tendons throughout the body are activated.

TENDON EXERCISES
All-Tendon Action

1. Start in Sink Back position with the hands in Push position.

Inhale: Feel the tendons absorb the Chi.

2. Advance slowly until you are almost fully forward.

3. Listen to the heart. Feel the blood rushing out to the extremities.

4. As you feel the blood pulsing outward, widen the eyes and concentrate the mind. The wave of expansion travels in a manner similar to that described in the Chi Transfer form. The movement is from the Tan Tien down to the ground.

1. Listen to your heart. 2. Widen the eyes and concentrate the mind.
3. Direct the Chi from the Tan Tien down to the earth.
4. Feel the Earth energy extend up the body. Open all the joints and feel the tendons stretch like rubber.

5. From the ground, the wave travels up through the feet, legs, spine, arms, and hands. The emphasis is on being aware of the tendons and ligaments and feeling their connection to the mind, eye, and heart. Feel like rubber.

6. Once the wave reaches the hands, the tendon stretch causes the fingers to gently separate and straighten. The expansion and contraction of the body is related to Chi flow. The Chi expands into the hand as the tendons are stretched.

7. During the subsequent contraction, Chi is drawn in.

First draw in the Chi.

As the tendons twist and stretch, the fingers open and extend. Practicing lengthening the index finger will help open the whole arm joint.

This form is thus related to the Yin and Yang form, which describes the process of exchanging Chi or energy with the environment. The ability to connect to the earth and draw up Earth energy is basic to the Tendon Activation form. Also, the movement of the spinal cord (learned in the Chi Transfer form) exercises the flexible tendons in the spine to accomplish the "wave" on which the Chi travels. The following form, the Tan Tien form, combines the essence of all the organs to form a pearl of energy whose movement directs the movement of the rest of the body.

ACTIVATING THE TENDONS IN TAI CHI CHI KUNG
Introductory Movements
Wu Chi Stance

The most important part of this stance, beyond the proper alignment of structure to facilitate tendon action, is the coordination between the Chi pulse that is flowing through the tendons and both the breath and the heart-

Wu-Chi Stance. Feel the pulse in the heart, palms and soles, mid-eyebrow, crown, and perimeum. Feel all the joints opening and expanding.

beat. The pulse can be initially sensed at the palms, mid-eyebrow, crown, perineum, and soles of the feet. However, after an initial sensitization to the pulse timing, the attention should be placed on the joints of the wrists, elbows, hips, knees, and ankles to feel these activation points open up.

Breathing rhythmically, in combination with smiling to the body with a mental emphasis on opening the joints, both relaxes the practitioner and prepares the tendons to be utilized as guides for the Chi energy assimilated during the practice.

Opening Tai Chi

Once again, the importance of letting the weight of the body be supported by the tendons as opposed to the muscles cannot be overemphasized. The best signal to the practitioner that the tendons are being properly utilized is lack of muscle fatigue. At first, the tendons may actually ache from lack of previous use; however, after a short time, flexibility and strength is greatly enhanced by relying on the tendons for all the Tai Chi actions.

Core Movements

Grasping the Bird's Tail: North

In this portion of the form, most of the tendon areas of emphasis have been brought out in the description of the Yin/Yang and Rooting forms. However, now you should concentrate on the degree of tendon rotation and the efficiency of energy recovery and transfer out of the body from the tendons during the Yang release phase.

First Ward Off: Holding the Chi Ball

During the weight transfer, pay careful attention to the tendons in the hip, knee, and ankle of the supporting leg. Let the leg muscles entirely relax as the tendons guide the weight to the ground.

Second Ward Off: Holding the Chi Ball

During this first outward-directed action, concentrate on the springing action of the tendons that guide the responding Earth energy up the legs through the body to the spine, scapulae, and arms. Specifically, the tendon points of action are the ankles, knees, hips, shoulders, elbows, and wrists. As your concentration improves, you can incorporate the knuckles of the toes and fingers as well as the collar bone.

Rollback

The tendon action here is contained in the knee, which leads the action of the hips, which

Femur

Fibula Tibia

The spiraling of the knee joint.

carries the upper body as one unit. As the knee moves, the feet remain in position, and the tendons wrap from the ankle to the knee. This action should be felt and maximized during the practice. Feel the additional twisting action as the knee is moved before the hip, wrapping the tendons around the femur (the thigh bone).

Then, with the groin opened, the hip begins to move, creating a twisting action in the tendons that run up the side of the body. At maximum extension, finally, the upper body follows until the navel points at 90 degrees (to the West).

Two Hand Press

The same considerations described for the Second Ward Off apply to the Two Hand Press.

Two Hand Push

As with the Two Hand Press, the same considerations that were described for the Second Ward Off apply to the Two Hand Push.

Single Whip: South

Single Whip involves the Triple Twist. This means that it is also tendon intensive in its application. Here a force is generated by wrapping the tendons around the entire length of the body (rotational motion).

Pivot

Transfer the weight to the tendons of the back leg to support the entire body. Once again, as in Rollback, the knee that is turning the body leads as it wraps the tendon around the lower leg from the ankle. At full rotational extension, the tendon of the femur is then fully wrapped.

Making the Beak

The hip then moves to create a twisting action on the right side of the body, where the upper body follows to a full turn to the right. Here too, the weight is transferred to the opposite leg; this requires a smooth transition from one set of tendons to the other so that the motion is slow and graceful. The twisting action of the legs during the creation of the beak is identical, but in the opposite direction. However, the arms and the bent wrist of the beak add an upper-body tendon contraction from the shoulders to the elbows, wrists, and fingers of the beak hand.

In turning, transfer the weight to the tendons on the back of the legs.

Releasing the Beak

In this portion of the practice, the fruits of the newly strengthened tendons and fully coiled body can be tested as an effective weapon. When the action is slow, the attention to the release and extension of the tendons provides realization of the power that the beak release contains.

Tendon power releases when turning.

Reaching Up to Heaven

During this portion, be sure that the motion of the tendons of both legs and arms are not rushed, and that the Yang action initiated in Releasing the Beak is carried over into the next motion of the Single Hand Push via the tendons.

Single Hand Push

The tendon functions here are identical to those of the Second Ward Off.

Transition to a New Direction

Holding the Baby

When you hold a baby—which is done most efficiently with the tendons of the arms as well as the legs—the actions need to be smooth and graceful. This should be the concern during this portion of the practice, letting the tendons be powerful yet gentle.

Right Hand Form

The actions of the tendons of the Right Hand Form are the same as described above except that they occur on the opposite side. In Tai Chi, all the tendons must be equally exercised to Change the Tendons, so that the weaker tendons become equal to the stronger.

Concluding Movements

At the end of the Tai Chi form, the energy must be collected in the tendons and directed in a circulation that collects the trapped areas of residue. This energy can then be guided via both the tendons and the Microcosmic Orbit to the navel center for storage during the final Hun Yuan spiraling.

11
The Tan Tien Form

All movement in Tai Chi originates from the Tan Tien. This important region is responsible for control and balance, two key ingredients in proper Tai Chi execution. Additionally, the Chi generated through Tai Chi practice is stored in the Tan Tien; this energy then becomes a reserve that you can add to each time you practice.

While the Tan Tien is both the source and container of Chi power, the mind acts like a general that issues orders to the Tan Tien for directing the power, and the Tan Tien is like the army camp that dispatches the troops. To be successful with the Tan Tien form, the mind must be strengthened and focused, and the Tan Tien must filled with Chi pressure.

The mind's ability to focus and to actually move the Chi is enhanced by meditation. The Microcosmic Orbit meditation, Iron Shirt, Healing Love, and Tai Chi all involve generating, storing, and circulating Chi. It is essential at the end of these practices to collect the energy in the Tan Tien. If the energy is stored in the Tan Tien, it can be accessed later; if not, the Chi dissipates and cannot be used. Storing the Chi is accomplished by spiraling at the navel during the final Hun Yuan Stance.

We usually refer to the lower abdominal area as the Tan Tien, but we actually have three Tan Tiens: the lower Tan Tien, the middle Tan Tien (heart), and the upper Tan Tien (behind the mid-eyebrow point). Of the three Tan Tiens, all used in Taoist inner alchemy, the lower Tan Tien is the most important in Tai Chi Chi Kung. The lower Tan Tien (henceforth referred to as "the Tan Tien"), is located in the abdomen approximately three finger-widths below the navel toward the center of the body. The precise location varies from person to person and depends on body type. The Tan Tien stores our Original Chi. Original Chi is the Chi derived from the egg and sperm of our parents, from which our entire organism arises.

Taoist practices emphasize developing and circulating the Chi. The Tan Tien is also called the ocean of Chi. According to Chinese medical theory, once the ocean is full, it overflows into the eight extraordinary meridians. Once these are full, the Chi flows into the twelve ordinary meridians, each of which is associated with a particular organ. The Tan Tien, then, is clearly the foundation of the entire energetic system.

The Tan Tien form strengthens both the mind and the fasciae to give the practitioner a way of quickly and effectively drawing energy from one area and directing it to another. This skill is particularly useful in other Taoist practices, such as Healing Love, where the energy may be pulling strongly in an undesirable direction (out of the body).

Another way energy can leak out of the body is through urination. With the Tan Tien practice, if a Chi ball is formed and raised away from the bladder area during urination, this indiscriminate loss of energy can be greatly reduced.

As a result of its capacity to deal with large amounts of Chi, the Tan Tien was used as a "laboratory" for Inner Alchemical work. Translated from the Chinese, the word Tan means elixir (literally cinnabar, a mineral used in Outer Alchemy as the basis for the elixir of immortality, as it was considered to have the perfect balance of Yin and Yang); Tien means field or place. The elixir, also known as "the pearl," was formed in the Tan Tien by combining the energies of all the systems of the body, including the organs, glands, and senses. The Fusion of the Five Elements meditation gives precise instructions for forming the pearl.

PRELIMINARY TAN TIEN EXERCISES
Tan Tien Breathing

1. Stand in Horse Stance, arms curved, palms facing the Tan Tien.
2. Be aware of the palms and soles. Shoot energy into the navel from the palms as if they were two lasers.

3. Feel the Tan Tien begin to expand. Allow the hands to expand away from the body as the Tan Tien expands.
4. Pull the lower abdomen in, condensing the energy in the Tan Tien. The hands are drawn closer to the body as the navel is drawn in.
5. Feel as though you had a Chi ball in the belly. As you inhale, feel the Chi ball expand. As you exhale, feel the Chi ball contract and condense.
6. Continue breathing in/expanding and breathing out/condensing 20 to 30 times, until you feel the Chi ball become quite substantial.

Expanding the Chi ball.

Leading Your Movements from the Tan Tien

1. Step forward into Bow and Arrow Stance with the right foot, keeping the weight on the back leg.
2. Then shift forward by pressing into the ground with the left foot and feeling the

Pushing forward the Chi ball.

ground force come up and expand the Chi ball.

3. Shift back to the left foot, feeling that the Chi ball is leading the movement by contracting.

Sinking back the Chi ball.

4. Turn to the left, leading the movement with the turning of the Chi ball at the Tan Tien.

Turning the Chi ball.

You should be able to feel that the Chi ball in the Tan Tien initiates and leads all your movements, whether forward or back, left or right, diagonally upward or diagonally downward.

Working with the Tan Tien in Tai Chi Chi Kung
Introductory Movements
Wu Chi Stance

During this portion of the practice, you will create a Chi ball in the Tan Tien, which will then be moved around during the form. To

assist in creating the Chi ball, smiling is very important. Just as the pearl is created in the Fusion meditation, the glands and organs must relax and release their energies so that the mind can direct them to the Tan Tien. There they can be used as a powerful virtue force for healing and exchanging energy with the environment.

Divide the Chi ball and press it down the legs. This will make you feel rooted.

To create a bucket-like storage area for the energy you release as you relax, lower the thoracic diaphragm to create a pressing action on the Tan Tien. This action pushes the Chi ball down as you simultaneously gently pull up the sexual organs and anus. The pressure from above and below compacts and fills the Chi ball in the Tan Tien.

When you relax, the Earth energy will rise up the Tan Tien.

When you are ready to begin the form, divide the Chi ball in two, sending one part down each leg into the ground to establish better rooting. Once you are rooted, draw in Earth energy by bringing the two halves back up the legs to the Tan Tien and reunite them to reform the Chi ball.

Opening Tai Chi

1. After stepping out, reestablish your connection to the ground. Concentrate on the additional power that the Chi ball gives to the structure while raising the arms. Move the Chi ball forward and expand it to the front while performing the first Two Hand Push. Feel the energy both pulling up force from the ground through the legs and pushing out force through the arms to the palms. Expand the Tan Tien area not only in the front but at the sides and lower back as well, as if you had a beach ball in the abdomen.

Move the Chi ball from the navel to the arm.

2. As you draw back and lower the arms, sink down and push the Chi ball down toward the coccyx, sacrum, and perineum.

When lowering the arms, draw the energy through the arms and bring it to the Tan Tien.

When the arms are down, push the Chi ball to the coccyx.

3. This creates an emptiness above the Chi ball that can be filled by Chi newly drawn through the arms during this Yin phase. It also creates a better connection with the earth.

Core Movements – Left Hand Form

As you transition the weight during the subsequent turns, the Chi ball is moved to the side of the turn; this acts to massage the left kidney, spleen, stomach, pancreas, and descending colon when turning to the left, and the liver, gall bladder, and ascending colon when turning to the right. Each transition passes the Chi ball over the small intestines and transverse colon, massaging them as well.

The Tan Tien form differentiates between the Left Hand form and the Right Hand form only by the side of the body toward which the Chi ball is passed. This becomes self-evident in the course of practice, and therefore only one corner of action is described.

Grasping the Bird's Tail: North

First Ward Off: Holding the Chi Ball

During this portion of the form, as the hands rotate and you sink back into a Yin phase, move the Chi ball back against the spine to massage the kidneys.

Second Ward Off: Holding the Chi Ball

As the hips turn to the right, pass the Chi ball to the right side to press on the right kidney. Then, as you begin the Yang forward Ward Off motion, move the Chi ball to the front right side, pressing on the right side of the bladder and sexual center. This enables the outward motion of energy to proceed from the Tan Tien up to the arms and out through the palms.

Rollback

During the sink back portion, lower the Chi ball toward the coccyx, sacrum, and perineum;

this creates a void that will be filled by energy newly drawn in through the fingers and palms of the hands, down the arms to the navel. Reinforce the turn to the left side with the motion of the Chi ball toward the back and left kidney; this also draws in additional energy from the raised right hand.

Single Whip: South

First Twist

Once again, pass the Chi ball back in the direction of the pivot; this creates a massaging action on the central internal organs of the body. It reaches the left kidney with a gentle squeezing action as you reach maximum extension.

Press

As you return the Chi ball to the front of the body for the Press, press it toward the bladder and sexual center, creating a connection between the ground and the direction of force.

Two Hand Push

The Two Hand Push has the same Chi ball motion as in Press. Assist this forward and backward motion of the Chi ball with the sacrum tilting action that was described in the previous chapters.

Second Twist: Making the Beak

Pass the Chi ball back to the right kidney as you form the beak. Again, the Chi ball reaches the right kidney with a gentle squeezing action as you reach maximum extension.

Third Twist: Releasing the Beak

As you release the beak, pass the Chi ball back to the front of the body and begin the Yang action of pressing down to the bladder and sexual center to connect the Earth energy to the new outward motion of the force.

Reaching Up to Heaven

Bring the Chi ball from the right side of the sexual center and bladder to the center, creating the same connection with the ground, now equally distributed over both legs.

Single Hand Push

Bring the Chi ball to the left side of the sexual center and bladder. This completes the Yang action by providing the additional Earth force directed out the arm to the palm of the left hand.

Transition to a New Direction

Each of the corners is performed with the Tan Tien in exactly the same motion as described above for the North direction. For brevity, the description is not repeated.

Holding the Baby

Pass the Chi ball from the front of the body in the area of the sexual center and bladder to the back of the spine in the sacrum and coccyx region, and then back to the front of the body. Again, this action both reinforces and is reinforced by the sacral action. It is also a powerful means of drawing additional energy into the void created by pressing the Chi ball low into the body; use the upward-turned palms to draw in this additional energy.

Right Hand Form

As mentioned earlier, there is no difference between the Left Hand form and the Right Hand form except that the Chi ball is on the opposite side.

CONCLUDING MOVEMENTS
Cross Hands and Closing Tai Chi

During the action of crossing the hands and returning to the Wu Chi Stance, re-center the Chi ball into the exact middle of the body from whence it came, to the center of balance, center of gravity, and center of attention. This brings the practice to completion.

Hun Yuan Stance

In the Tan Tien form, the Hun Yuan Stance is very important. Stand relaxed with the feet together, left palm over the right palm over the navel. Direct the total attention to the navel and spiral the energy into the Tan Tien.

The importance of gathering and storing the energy cannot be overemphasized. With all the effort and enjoyment of doing the practice, it would be a shame to let all the results leak out by not taking the last step of locking up the energy in the Tan Tien.

Use the mind and spiral in the Tan Tien to collect energy.

Avoid eating or going to the bathroom for 45 minutes after Tai Chi practice. All the energy is concentrated in the navel area, and it would be greatly decreased by the digestion and excretion processes, both of which use up a great deal of energy.

12
The Healing Form

CONNECTING THE ORGANS WITH THE FIVE DIRECTIONS
Draw the Chi of the Five Directions

An important element in learning the Tai Chi form is sensitivity toward the directional energies. The Inner Smile can help the student in knowing what the feeling of healthy energy is like, in order to draw the complementary energies from the various directions. The following is a list of these directions and the corresponding major, minor and sensory organs:

1. North - water element - the energy of the kidneys, bladder, and ears.
2. South - fire element - the energy of the heart, small intestine, and tongue.
3. East - wood element - the energy of the liver, gall bladder, and eyes.
4. West - metal element - the energy of the lungs, large intestines, and the nose.
5. Middle - the Earth element - the energy of the spleen, stomach, pancreas, and mouth.

The way we move in our environment determines our exposure to each of the directions, North, South, East, and West (the Chinese have a fifth direction, the Center). Our houses are fixed in terms of compass orientation. We usually sit in the same chair facing the same direction at the table during meals; we favor a particular chair in which we spend most of the evening hours; we sleep with our body aligned in a particular direction, be it North-South, or East-West. When we get out of bed in the morning, we always head in the same direction to go to the bathroom; the door through which we exit the house always opens to the same direction; the path leading to the car is invariable. We typically take the quickest route to work. At work, our office is on one side of the building, and the desk faces one direction. We drive home along the same route to return to a house which has not shifted while we were gone (unless it is in California).

Constrained by our activities within a fixed environment, most of us are overexposed to certain directions and underexposed to others. As the pattern of the typical day is repeated over the course of weeks, months, and years, this overexposure to certain directions and underexposure to others is compounded.

Each direction is associated with a distinctive type of energy. Balance and harmony are achieved through maintaining equal proportions of each of these energies. To achieve this goal, the movements in Tai Chi Chi Kung are practiced facing all the directions. In the Healing form, the energy from the four directions and the center are drawn into their associated organs. If you can get in touch with the energy of the five directions every day, you can maintain and strengthen the functioning of your organs. If you do get sick, by connecting with these energies you can heal faster.

The organs also have color, animal, and planet associations. The colors and animals are symbolic of the energy of the directions. Their efficacy in evoking the energies has been made available to us as tools passed down by innumerable Taoist meditators. Using these same colors and animals helps connect with the associated energies with which the adepts worked.

The same cosmic particles that formed the planets also form the organs. In this sense, the planets are considered parents of the organs. The organs' energies can be nurtured by the energy of their "parent" planets.

You can also see the division of the levels of the Healing form in terms of Earth level, Human or Cosmic level, and Heaven level. At the Earth level practice, you will use the directional forces, animals, and colors to tune into their associated energies. These energies are drawn into the body through the palms, soles, and perineum.

At the Human or Cosmic level practice, you will use the Six Healing Sounds and the Chi ball to tune into the associated energies. These energies are drawn into the body from in front through the mid-eyebrow.

At the Heaven level, you will use the planets and their colors to tune into the associated energies. These energies are drawn into the body through the crown. Here is a table of the associations.

You must master all the previous levels of Tai Chi Chi Kung before advancing to the Healing form. When you have reached this level, rooting, spiraling, Yin and Yang, tendons, structure, and the other Tai Chi principles will have already become so integrated into your form that you will not have to think about them; they will just happen by themselves, so you are free to relax and absorb the healing energy.

Direction	North	East	South	West	Center
Element	Water	Wood	Fire	Metal	Earth
Energy	Storing	Expanding	Releasing	Gathering	Balanced
Yin Organ	Kidneys	Liver	Heart	Lungs	Spleen & Pancreas
Yang Organ	Bladder	Gall Bladder	Small Intestine	Large Intestine	Stomach
Color	Blue	Green	Red	White	Yellow - Golden
Animal	Blue Tortoise	Green Dragon	Red Pheasant	White Tiger	Golden Phoenix
Planet	Mercury	Jupiter	Mars	Venus	Saturn

It is also important that you have experience with the Advanced level of the Fusion of the Five Elements meditation. This meditation acquaints the practitioner with the various directional energies and their associated colors, planets, and animals.

When first practicing the Healing form, simply concentrate on the organ associated with each direction. Look up the organs in an anatomy book; know what they look like and what their functions are. Then during the form, you can easily visualize the organ. Practicing the Inner Smile and Six Healing Sounds will also give you familiarity with the location of the organs and their energy.

In subsequent repetitions of the form, concentrate on only one association per organ: color, then animal, then planet. Breathe the color in. Picture the animal coming to you. Picture the planet, and feel its energy being absorbed into you. After gaining familiarity with the associations in this way, you may combine all the associations into one form.

It is also particularly helpful during the Healing form to incorporate the Six Healing Sounds based on the direction of the Grasping the Bird's Tail. This helps both tune the mind into the particular energy and stimulate the organ to a healing vibration that will release the negative trapped energies and nurture the virtue energies of the respective organs.

PRACTICE: THE HEALING FORM

Without repeating the specifics of the Tai Chi Chi Kung form itself, here is a summary of the energies of the Earth, Cosmic, and Heaven levels of the Healing form combined. You can divide the practice to work up to the combined Healing form, or you can work with whatever is most apparent at first while developing the more subtle energies next. The most important thing to remember about this form is that it is to be used for total mind and body health. Therefore, proper mental attitude and virtuous emotional control are essential.

When facing a particular direction during the Tai Chi Chi Kung form, absorb energy into the associated organs. Move the Tan Tien and Chi ball to massage that organ. During the

course of one complete form, you will thus activate all the organs.

Wu Chi Stance

Using the Wu Chi Stance to smile to the heart fosters a total body feeling of love, joy, and happiness that sets the tone for your healing practice.

North

You begin the Tai Chi Healing form facing North. On the North side, the kidneys and bladder connect with the Water element, the Earth force, and the Blue Turtle. Energetically, the North Direction connects with the North Star, the planet Mercury, and with the gathering and conserving energy phase.

Facing North: Nourish the kidneys with the North Star energy.

Smile and be aware of your kidneys and bladder. Feel the Watery quality of gathering and conserving being drawn into you. The bones and teeth are also connected with the North side (as they are ruled by the kidneys), so when you collect energy, bring it into them. Draw the blue color and the Turtle to you from the Earth force on the Northern horizontal plane.

When you sink back, push the Chi ball back into both kidneys. Press into the kidneys using your mind and a slight contraction of the stomach. When you roll back to the left, press into the left kidney, squeezing it. When you roll back to the right, press the right kidney. When you relax, the kidney expands, drawing more life force into it.

The energy of Mercury comes from above. Mercury supplies the kidneys with power. Add the energy of the planet Mercury to the bladder and kidneys. Picture the blue color of Mercury; feel its healing power strengthening your kidneys, bladder, and bones.

West

The West side connects with the lungs and large intestine, which are associated with elimination. The energy of the West is associated with the Metal element, a very condensed form of energy. When we take this energy into the lungs, we get courage.

The associated color is white. When you can visualize these organs as you do the form, you receive more healing.

Smile to the lungs, and feel a white force from the West coming to you. Summon a White Tiger on the West side to give you more energy.

Feel the Chi ball moving. When you sink the chest and empty the lungs, you can breathe into the back of the lungs and lower abdomen.

When facing West, draw the energy of the White Tiger in the West into the lungs.

When you have a good connection with the West, connect with the Heaven force, the planet Venus. Picture the planet, and be aware of the white force coming down. This requires mind power. Emphasize sinking the chest and emptying the lungs when you push out.

South

The South side connects with the force of Fire. The energy is expanding and radiant and helps the heart and the blood circulation.

Smile to the heart. Feel the expanding, radiating energy of love. When you feel joyful and happy, expanding and radiant, you will feel wonderful all over. Smile to the heart and small intestine. The red color is very important for both the heart and small intestine. Fire is needed to digest food. The heart also needs fire to move the blood.

From the South draw the Fire energy of the Red Pheasant into your heart.

When you do the form facing South, feel the heart radiating a red color. Sink the sternum and be aware of the heart. Call the power of the Red Pheasant, the animal of the South, to strengthen and protect you on the South side.

Expand your consciousness out and be aware of the planet Mars. Absorb its red color from above down into the heart.

East

The East is connected with the liver and gall bladder. The color is green. The energy is expansive and growing, like a tree. The tendons are also connected with the East.

Facing East, draw the green energy of the Wood element into the liver.

When you roll back, press and massage the liver with the Chi ball. Learn to use the Tan Tien, where the Original Force is stored. When you sink, you come back to the Center and press against the spleen. Emphasize sinking back, pressing into the liver and gall bladder.

Call the Green Dragon, the animal of the East.

Be aware of the planet Jupiter. This planet has a tremendous amount of energy that can benefit the liver and gall bladder.

Center

The Center is associated with the spleen, pancreas, stomach, and Earth force. The balanced, harmonizing energy of the Center can best be absorbed from the Sink Back, Wu Chi, and Hun Yuan closing positions. No matter which direction you are facing, when you sink back, connect with and absorb the yellow energy. Draw the Yellow Phoenix to you, over your head.

In sinking back, absorb the yellow energy
of the Center into the spleen and stomach.

Connect with the yellow healing light of the planet Saturn. When you sink down, press the spleen and pancreas with the Chi ball.

13

The Skin and Bone Breathing Form

Since the skeletal framework is the foundation and core of our physical structure, to master Tai Chi Chi Kung one must learn to activate, energize and transform the bones and marrow.

For centuries, Chinese martial artists have integrated various Chi Kung practices into their training to exercise and develop the bones. In the Healing Tao we introduce these practices within the context of Iron Shirt Chi Kung and Bone Marrow Nei Kung (Iron Shirt Chi Kung III). Within Iron Shirt, the main practices that focus on activating the bones are Bone Breathing, Skin Breathing, and Marrow Washing.

Bone Breathing in the Embracing the Tree posture of Iron Shirt Chi Kung.

In all these practices, we draw energy into the bones. This removes fat from the bone marrow and creates space for the marrow to grow, enhancing our ability to produce healthy blood cells.

Yellow Marrow (Fat)

Prolonged Bone Breathing practice helps to clear the fat from the bones, nurturing the regrowth of the red marrow.

The blood cells, in turn, nourish the body and help it resist disease. The marrow of round bones, such as those of the arms, legs, and spine, produces red blood cells. The red blood cells carry oxygen and nutrients to all the cells in the body. The marrow of flat bones such as the skull, ribs, and hips produces white blood cells, the soldiers of the immune system.

Healthy blood is thus essential for a healthy body.

These practices also strengthen the bone matrix. The strength of the matrix is in essence the structural strength of the bones. Bone matrix is the main storehouse of calcium in the body. The bone matrix also stores Chi in an unusual way: bone is one of the few substances on Earth other than quartz crystal that has piezo-electrical properties. This means that the electrical charge of the bones increases in proportion to the pressure exerted on the bones.

Tai Chi Chi Kung is one of the best exercises in the world for pressurizing the bones, because we emphasize shifting the load-bearing job from the muscles to the bones in each and every movement. In addition, we align our entire skeletal structure so that the mechanical force generated in each movement passes through all of the bones. The pressure generated enlivens and activates the energy stored in the bone.

The cells making up the bone matrix tissue are some of the liveliest cells in the body. The bone tissue cells align to each other according to the type of force to which they are subjected. In Tai Chi Chi Kung, the bones are subjected to a simultaneous vertical and horizontal force, which manifests as a spiral. The result is that the bone cells form into a densely woven spiral lattice pattern, creating incredibly tough bones.

Taoists believe the cosmic particles we absorb through Skin and Bone Breathing build up our bodies, cells, and organs. As we draw these particles in, we immediately increase our energy. In Tai Chi Chi Kung, we are concerned with the more basic bone training techniques. My previous books, Iron Shirt Chi Kung I and Bone Marrow Nei Kung, give in-depth information on both the bone breathing process and the additional techniques for reinforcing the Chi in the bone marrow.

Although Bone Breathing, Skin Breathing and Marrow Washing all exercise the bone marrow, they do so in different ways. Actually, all of these exercises are often subsumed under the name of bone breathing; in the context of this chapter, we refer to them as something separate.

Stage One: Respiration through the fingers. In the beginning stages of Bone Breathing, the mind and the eyes are used to draw and absorb the external energy.

1. Using the mind and eyes, breathe in through the finger tips.

2. Direct the energy to the head, then bring it down to the middle of the back. With practice, you will direct it all the way down the legs to the feet.

Stages two and three: Respiration through the toes and simultaneous practice.

In the second stage of Bone Breathing, inhale through the toes up into the thigh bones, sacrum, and up the spine.

In the third stage, simultaneously breathe in through the fingers and toes.

In Bone Breathing, we use the power of our mind to establish a flow of external Chi through the fingertips, toes, and the other protruding bones of the body, spreading it throughout the skeletal structure.

In Skin Breathing, the hundred thousand pores and hair follicles in the skin draw in energy from the atmosphere. Hair follicles and pores are the most sensitive part of the body in terms of attracting ions, electrons and protons in the air. The movement of electrical charge within the body underlies all metabolic processes. On the inbreath we draw the Chi in through the pores and follicles down to the surface of the bone; on the outbreath, we condense the Chi into the bones by contracting the muscles close to the bone. We also refer to this process as bone compression.

1. Spiraling the energy

2. Breathe Chi from the outside in, packing around the bones

3. Squeezing the energy into the bones

Skin Breathing and Bone Breathing are efficient supplements to breathing through the nose. The surface area of the skin is far greater than that of the nose alone and therefore has greater energy drawing potential.

Marrow Washing is a more passive process. Although we draw in external Chi as we do in the previous practices, unlike bone and skin breathing, this absorption is not coordinated with our breathing. We open ourselves to receive the downward flow of Chi from Heaven through our crown and palms, the upward flow of Chi from Earth through our palms, soles and perineum, and the horizontal flow of atmospheric or Cosmic Chi through our mid-eyebrow point. Eventually we absorb Chi through all of the skin into the bones, and the practices of Skin Breathing and Marrow Washing blend together. The energy in Marrow Washing is very gentle, like a fine mist of light that steam cleans and energizes our bone marrow with Yin, Yang and neutral energies.

BASIC EXERCISES
Marrow Washing, Bone and Skin Breathing

1. Take a very simple stance, the Heavenly Stance, with the feet parallel, knee-to-toe-length apart. The arms are raised over the head, elbows bent, palms facing up.

2. Use your mind to draw the Heavenly force in. It may appear in your mind's eye as a violet light mist emanating from the North Star. Draw the energy in through your crown and palms and into the bones. Feel the violet mist wash through your bone marrow from top to bottom.

Absorbing Heavenly Force.

3. Lower the hands so that they are in front at waist level with palms facing down. This is the Earthly Stance.

4. Draw up the energy from the earth, the negative charge from Mother Earth, through the soles of your feet, perineum and palms. The Earth energy may appear to your mind's eye as a yellow mist. Feel it wash through your bones as if it were steam cleaning them.

Absorbing Earth Force.

5. When you feel the Heavenly and Earth forces and have brought them to the navel, focus the awareness on the skin. You can use your hands to lightly rub your skin. Feel the sensations on the skin surface.

6. Inhale, and draw the Chi from the atmosphere--ions, protons, electrons, particles of light--into the skin and down to the outer surface of your bones. Feel your hair follicles acting like lightning rods or antennae, attracting and drawing the energy in.

7. Exhale, lightly contract the muscles closest to the bone, and squeeze the Chi into the bone. Feel it condense into the bones, charging them up. Your bones will feel full, expanded and distended, electric.

By inhaling through the fingertips and skin, packing, spiraling, and squeezing energy into the bones, an electrical impulse is created.

8. Inhale again. Be aware of the kidneys and the sexual center; these centers help absorb particles into the bone to regrow the marrow. Exhale a little bit. Rest, relax your breathing and feel the skin breathing by itself for six to nine breaths.

Heaven and Earth Marrow Washing

1. Lower the arms and keep them rounded, palms up, as if you are scooping the energy up from the earth.

2. Inhale, and feel the Earth energy come up to the soles and the perineum. Slightly contract the anus and inhale energy up to the sacrum. Inhale up to T- 11, pushing out the spine slightly. Continue in the same way to T-5, C-7, the base of the skull, and the crown.

3. Be aware of the Big Dipper and the North Star above you. Inhale. You may feel something very heavy in the crown. Use the Heavenly energy to wash the bone marrow. Exhale down. Rest, and just feel

the positive Heavenly charge wash down through the brain, skull, cervical vertebrae, clavicle, and sternum.

4. Draw the energy down through the rib cage and activate the marrow that produces the white blood cells. Draw the energy down the thoracic and lumbar vertebrae to the hips and leg bones. Feel the violet light washing right through the bones. Just rest and breathe softly, and let the process happen by itself.

Breathing into the collarbone, sternum, and ribs.

5. Rest and continue breathing gently. Be aware of your soles and palms, and feel the yellow light rising from the earth; let it wash the bone marrow from the legs up to the sacrum, to the spine (lumbar, thoracic, cervical), to the brain, and up. (The hands have gradually been raised above the head.)

6. Do the exercise 10 to 20 times.

Solar Marrow Washing

Sunlight, especially morning sunlight (visualized as violet and yellow), activates bone marrow energy. You can train by looking at the sun right at dawn, before its light is too bright.

1. Start by looking at the sun and blinking your eyes rapidly. Then close your eyes. When you close your eyes, you can see violet and yellow. Single out those colors and absorb the energy into the skin and bones.

2. Inhale into the bones and exhale. Relax. Do this for a few minutes until you feel you have learned the process. Once you

have learned the process, the absorption of energy can take place automatically.

Absorb the Sun's Energy.

3. Yellow light from the sun comes down into the bone marrow, washing. it, increasing it, strengthening it. Sometimes when you look at the sun, you see the red light also. The bones need this too. Visualize that light. Absorb the light in through the mid-eyebrow, mouth, and skin on the inbreath; condense and draw it in to wash the marrow by lightly contracting the muscles near the bone on the outbreath.

The Bone Marrow Inner Smile

After performing the Heaven and Earth Marrow Washing, stand for a while and smile to the entire skeletal structure. Take your time to smile to each bone one by one.

1. Smile to the skull.

2. Smile to each cervical vertebra. Feel the Chi penetrate into each cervical vertebra, filling and expanding the intravertebral space.

3. Smile to the collarbone, scapulae, humerus, radius and ulna, and bones of the wrists and hands. Smile especially to the joints in between the bones; feel the Chi filling the joint space.

4. Smile down to the thoracic vertebrae, lumbar vertebrae, and pelvis. Feel the Chi filling and expanding the joint space.

5. Smile down to the groin (kua), and feel the Chi fill up the hip joint. Smile to your femur, one of the major bones responsible for producing red blood cells.

6. Continue smiling down to the knee joint, and feel the joint fill with Chi; smile to your tibia and fibula bones and the bones and joints of the ankles and feet.

7. Rest a moment and feel the entire skeletal structure.

INCORPORATE SKIN AND BONE BREATHING INTO THE TAI CHI CHI KUNG FORM

Introductory Movements

In this portion of the form, it is important to take the time to feel all the bones in the body. It is very helpful to look at an anatomy book to familiarize yourself with the look of the following skeletal bones: skull, spinal cord, upper and lower arms and legs, hands, feet, and hips. This allows more accurate visualization during the bone breathing process.

The Skeletal Structure.

After having become intimately aware of the entire skeleton, move the attention to the heart and kidneys. This activates the spirit and

Bones are extremely porous and are always "breathing"

essence energy respectively. Relax. Feel that you can absorb the energy into yourself.

Inhale the energy into the palms, the fingers, and particularly the pores of the skin. It is helpful to view the bone breathing drawings to follow what you can now sense as a feeling.

Core Movements

In the Core Movements section of the Tai Chi Chi Kung form, which is comprised of Grasping the Bird's Tail and Single Whip in the various directions, the mind-eye-heart power, as learned in the Tendon form, is very important. During the Yin phase of each movement, you can inhale, draw energy into the skin, and absorb it down to the surface of the bones. The more you relax, the more you draw energy in. During the Yang phase you exhale and condense the Chi into the bones.

Use the bone structure and breath to reinforce the energy flow. Feel the skeletal structure constantly drawing and then compressing the energy into the marrow; picture the bones and smile to the bones during the entire form.

When you sink back, this is the Yin phase of the movement; begin the Bone Breathing by breathing in Chi through the tips of your fingers, palms, and mid-eyebrow. As you become more accomplished, you can also draw in through more areas and centers such as the crown, the tips of the toes, the legs, and the skin.

During the Yin phase of sinking back, begin the Bone Breathing by breathing in Chi through you fingertips.

When you shift forward, this is th Yang phase of the movement; exhale, and contract the muscles into the bones, squeezing and condensing the Chi into the bones. Feel the energy penetrate deeply into the bones. If you can picture the bones as porous, like a sponge, it helps this process greatly.

Draw in the Chi through both the fingertips and toes.

As you shift forward during the Yang phase, the bones of your whole body feel porous, like a sponge. Feel all the bones breathing, and use your mind to compress the Chi into the bones.

Once you have begun and activated the Bone Breathing process, you can use less effort. Just relax and feel yourself absorbing Chi through the fingertips, energy centers and skin during the inbreath, and feel the Chi condensing into the bones during the outbreath. Continue to be aware of this process throughout the whole Tai Chi form. Eventually you will use mostly the mind and very little contraction of the muscles to absorb the Chi into the bones.

You have to go very slowly at this advanced level of practice for it to be effective. Draw the energy into the points as shown in the illustration, slowly and smoothly, as if you are pulling silk from a cocoon; if you pull too strongly you will break the strand, and if you pull too weakly it will not come.

As previously mentioned, the kidneys rule the sexual organs and bones. The more you can smile into the kidneys and sexual organs, and the slower you go, the more effectively you can draw the energy in.

The yellow, violet, and red colors help rejuvenate the bone marrow. The more you relax with good structure, the more you can feel the Chi being absorbed. Feel the skin while drawing in and the bones while breathing out. Absorb the energy into the skin, into every pore and hair follicle; you can picture the skin as one big lung. Transfer the force through the spinal cord as described in the previous chapters.

Opening the joints during Bone Breathing is a powerful aid to absorbing Chi into the bones.

Be constantly aware of Yin (inhale) and Yang (exhale). Actually feel that you are swimming in an ocean of Chi, as if you have to push through the Chi to create the bone breathing action. When absorbing the Chi, you may feel that the Chi is very thick. Stay aware of your structure, the Tan Tien motion, and particularly your bones. This form requires a high level of awareness, because in addition to the regular lengthwise flow of Chi through the structure, there is also a cross-sectional motion of energy from the entire surface of the skin into the bones guided by the mind-eye-heart. In Tai Chi Chi Kung we thus develop a deeper and more profound awareness in movement.

Transition to a New Direction

During Holding the Baby and the Concluding Movements portion of the form move very slowly or stand still form while, so that you can really have a chance to feel the main process of working with the breath and energy centers. Draw energy in through the head hair, crown, and torso down the legs to the soles. Concentrate on all the points in the Microcosmic Orbit: the crown, mid-eyebrow, throat point, solar plexus, navel, sexual center, perineum, sacrum, Door of Life, T-1 1, T-5/T-6, C-7, and Jade Pillow. All these points absorb the energy with greater strength when you direct the attention to them.

Flush the whole body; with the newly collected energy so your bone marrow is cleansed throughout; your entire body is like a sponge to the external supply of Chi. That is particularly true during this form, because all your skin pores are open due to your mind-eye-heart awareness.

CLOSING MOVEMENTS

When you are ready to finish the form, smile again to your entire skeletal bone structure and then gather and collect Chi at your navel.

14
The Integrated Structure Form

The preceding forms have exposed all the aspects of the internal structure of Tai Chi Chi Kung. The Yin and Yang form introduced the Three Forces and stressed the importance of smiling and relaxation for their absorption. The alignment and use of the skeletal structure given in the Rooted form and the Chi Transfer form give one the ability to absorb and discharge large amounts of energy and to properly maintain a connection with the Heavenly and Earth sources. The Tendon Activation form teaches how the "I," the combination of Mind-Eye-Heart, moves the energy to move the body. The Tan Tien form shows how to originate movement in the center of the body.

The Healing form makes the energy of the five directions available to their associated organs. The Skin and Bone Breathing form is for absorbing Chi into the bones.

The Integrated Structure form combines all the internal structure, skeletal and energetic, introduced in previous chapters. Learning to use your mind correctly is critical to accomplishing Tai Chi Chi Kung. Meditations such as the Microcosmic Orbit and the Fusion of the Five Elements, in which you learn to control,

direct, condense, and draw your internal energy, are thus very important to Tai Chi Chi Kung. If people learn only Tai Chi without any sitting meditation, they will find it difficult to use the mind to concentrate the energy; there are just too many things to learn at one time. It is like teaching people to draw with the left and right hands and both feet all at the same time. It just cannot be handled all at once.

A major advantage of a short form such as Tai Chi Chi Kung is that it does not take a long time to learn. Consequently, you have more time to devote to the internal work. The first goal in Tai Chi is to get the outer form right and be able to execute it automatically. Once you get the outer form down, the real work is to learn to use energy in each posture. The internal work is what is unique about Tai Chi, what distinguishes it from the external forms of martial arts. Not learning the internal part of Tai Chi is like having an oyster without ever bothering to look inside for the pearl.

COCKING THE BOW

The internal structure allows the body to move as a unit. A cardinal principle of Tai Chi is to lead each movement with the body, not the hands. Many people tend to move their hands first, but the legs and hips should move first and carry the rest of the body. This applies to both shifting the weight forward and sinking back.

Sinking back is very important. When you sink back, the back leg bends like a bow preparing to shoot an arrow. We call this "storing energy." In Tai Chi, you must store the strength inside before you release it. If this is not done properly, it is like pulling the bow back only halfway before releasing the arrow; there is then no gathering of power at all.

Sinking back is like "pulling a bow".

Also, when you shift forward and back, you should try to stay level; try not to bob up and down, or you will not be able to connect with the Earth force.

In stepping out, don't bounce up.

Although this sounds very simple, it seems very difficult for some people because they are used to using their hands and arms in isolation from the rest of their bodies. When your hands move by themselves, you will become more tense and obstruct the Chi flow. When you move the whole body in a very relaxed and integrated way, it feels smooth and light yet is also incredibly powerful. In the Tai Chi Classics it says, "My hands do not move even half an inch [by themselves]." Elsewhere in the Tai Chi Classics it also says, "My hands are not my hands; my body is my hand." If you understand this, you grasp a major part of Tai Chi theory. Your hands are moved by your legs, spine, and tendons. While it may sometimes appear that just your hands are moving, it is really your tendons that are stretching out. This is part of what we call Changing the Tendons.

Because your whole upper body is stacked over your hips and legs, if your base moves, your body moves as a single controlled unit. When we use our hands and arms in isolation, eventually we segment ourselves into too many parts.

This is also true for your mind. You should seek to practice with one mind that rests centered in Wu Chi. If your mind wanders from thought to thought, it becomes weak and diffuse.

LEARN TO BE LIKE A CHILD

Studying Tai Chi is learning to be like a child again, in both body and mind. Children don't have much muscle, so they naturally move with structure. In this respect, a child is much more flexible than an adult who doesn't practice Tai Chi. The way of flexibility is through relaxation, and by feeling delight, joy, and happiness.

ABSORB AND DIRECT ENERGY

Tai Chi is usually practiced slowly. The slow, even pace gives you time to really refine and perfect your structure while moving through a wide variety of postures. Once your structure is correct throughout the form, you can then train your mind to manage your Chi.

In Tai Chi you use your mind to gather and direct energy into your body and then to transform that energy. Once you have learned to absorb and transform energy, you can expand your awareness down, out, and up. In this way you can expand your awareness further and further out, connecting with the Earth, Heavenly, and Cosmic energy, which you can then absorb and draw for your own use.

When you feel you can draw the energy around you, you will automatically be moving more slowly and peacefully. You feel light, joyful, alive, and you feel the life force. In Tai Chi, the more you relax and smile to yourself, the more you get in touch with what is within you, and thus the more you feel true delight. It's not as though you have to say to yourself, "Oh, I have to do Tai Chi again..."

I have done Tai Chi for many years, and I've come to a point where this is truly my pleasure time. I can do away with TV, with drinking, with all the so-called pleasures in life, but I cannot do away with practicing Tai Chi. Why is Tai Chi my pleasure time? Because when I practice Tai Chi I feel delight; I am energetic and happy, and I feel my own life force.

People want to watch TV or go to night clubs to drink and smoke because they are so bored with their lives. Why are they bored? They have no life force. They need something to stimulate them and give them what they think is more life force. But apparently they have the wrong idea. Instead of gathering more Chi, they are draining it out. We call this "losing energy pleasure."

To absorb energy, it is important to start with smiling. Feel relaxed, feel joy, feel lightness inside of you. Smile to your heart. Sink down and connect to Mother Earth. Feel that you are like a tree and extend yourself up to the heavens. Open your armpits. Feel you are branching out to absorb the energy all around you.

ACHIEVING ONENESS WITH THE UNIVERSE

In the Taoist system and the Tai Chi system, the ultimate goal is to achieve oneness with the Tao, oneness with nature. In Tai Chi you reflect this in your body and mind. When you move, you move as one; everything moves at once. Instead of having the hands first, followed by the body, followed by the legs, if you can move as one, your legs push you and your whole body moves simultaneously as a unit. Gradually your sense of oneness in the body will grow.

Not only does your body move in oneness, but your mind does as well. Keep your mind and intention completely focused on your movements. Don't allow your mind to wander and scatter into random thoughts about the past and future. Stay present. When you move forward, use your mental intention to move everything forward. When you extend your hand, extend your mind as well. "The mind leads and the Chi follows; the Chi leads and the body follows." Thus in Tai Chi we practice oneness of body, Chi, and mind.

When we connect to the worlds around us, below us, and above us from this inner oneness, we feel intimately connected with the universe. The *Tao Te Ching* says, "Carrying body and soul and embracing the one, can you avoid separation? Attending fully and becoming supple, can you be as a newborn babe?"

15

Steel Wrapped in Cotton: Martial Art Applications

In Tai Chi, there are eight forces, each of which can be used for self-defense. The forces common in self-defense applications are (1) push down, (2) push up, (3) deflect to the right, (4) deflect to the left, (5) spiral, (6) trap, (7) pull backward, and (8) create a forward force.

Each of these has practical applications in each of the eight specific components of movements in the form: (1) Ward Off; (2) Rollback; (3) Press; (4) Push; (5) Pull Down; (6) Split; (7) Elbow Strike; and (8) Shoulder Strike.

WARD OFF

As stated earlier, there are two types of Ward Off in the Tai Chi Chi Kung form: a Yin Ward Off (which is a Holding the Ball application) and a Yang Ward Off. Each of the eight forces can be used within these two components of Ward Off.

The Holding the Ball Ward Off is a good example of a trap. With both hands held in a receiving, Yin position, a kick or punch can be received and trapped into a locked position. Subsequently, since you have one leg free, a forward force can be generated with a kick.

Yin Ward Off (Holding the Ball)   Yang Ward Off

This is why it is so important in Tai Chi to learn to stand balanced on one leg; each time you step out and put 100 percent of the weight on one of your legs, keep in mind that your other leg is free for a sharp kick.

The Yang Ward Off also involves trapping the force, but with a Yang attack it can involve deflecting elbow to elbow, and then trapping by placing one hand under the chin and the other on the spine. The Ward Off here flexes the opponent's spine unnaturally and locks him or her into submission.

Redirect the opponent's force to the side.

With your right hand push the opponent's chin to break the neck structure, and simultaneously with your left hand pull his lumbar vertabrae toward you to break his spinal structure.

Breaking the structure and alignment is a major goal in Tai Chi applications.

In Tai Chi applications, there is no need for grabbing or holding to trap with the hands when dealing with an oncoming force; a light touch with the open palms is all that is needed.

This is called sticking hand energy, and involves a leveraging of the wrists and elbows.

In a typical attack situation, when your opponent's arm comes forward with a punch, you stick at the wrist level and apply the pull backward (keeping the opponent moving forward) at the level of the elbow. However, as in all martial arts, an attempt at something like sticking hands in a specific area is never guaranteed, and therefore the actions are always multiple combinations to split the oncoming force in a few different directions.

In Yin Ward Off, use sticking hand energy to break the opponent's wrist structure and elbow strength.

The whole objective in Tai Chi is not to allow the oncoming force to reach you. The body is at most only about a foot or two wide, so by using the eight forces to your advantage with well-rehearsed, graceful, and coordinated body movement, what was previously a threat now becomes an application of what has been practiced in form.

Through the use of Ward Off, the force is divided into components between the eight forces mentioned. For example, you can deflect an oncoming punch to the right, and at the same time trap the opponent's front leg with your own front leg. You can then follow with a short downward push and a strong upward spiraling push from the hip to finish. This is a truly a divide-and-conquer strategy.

Trap the opponent's front leg with your front leg, causing his knee to lock and hyperextend.

Ward Off Combinations

Combining Ward Off with Push or Press is done through the use of the same sequence: Ward Off, push down, and then apply Push or

Ward Off and Press

1. Combining Ward Off with Press: gently deflect your opponent's right punch to your right.

2. Once his force is neutralized, join your right palm to your left wrist.

3. Guide your opponent's force downward. Absorb your opponent's force into your rear leg, gathering energy for Press.

4. Release your stored energy from your rear leg and throw him back using Press. Your front leg can also attack and trap his leg simultaneously.

Press for the final assault. To protect yourself, all you need to worry about is an area around you of about one foot in diameter, so as to avoid the oncoming blow.

Ward Off and Push

1. Use Ward Off and Push to gently stick and deflect his right hand punch to the right side. Remember not to use force; you only need his punch to miss you by a foot or so.

2. As your opponent starts to retreat, begin your push with a downward movement to trap his arm against and his body.

3. Follow through with your Push, now directing him upward, using the spiraling force from your legs and spine.

ROLLBACK

In Rollback, again the trapping force is used to eliminate the oncoming punch. This is then followed by a Press and roll of the forearm on the opponent's elbow, coordinated with a spiraling force from the hips, which rotates the opponent until he goes down with his shoulder locked.

The Rollback can also be used in combination with the sinking motion, to just avoid the oncoming punch. This gentle self-defense move allows the blow to be diverted and sends the opponent past you by his own force.

A more severe application of the Rollback would be to pull the opponent down as if you were cracking a whip (his arm), to send a wave motion up the arm to the shoulder area. This would usually lodge its full force at the cervical or lumbar vertebrae, causing a great amount of irreparable damage.

The seriousness of this counter is similar to the one mentioned above, where there is one hand under the chin and the other is on the spine, which causes an abnormal deflection of the vertebrae. The degree of damage inflicted and the seriousness of the counterattack varies from harmless to lethal in Tai Chi applications.

PRESS

Press is well illustrated by the K'an trigram of the *I Ching*, or *Book of Change*: Yang within and Yin without. K'an symbolizes danger, like the proverbial wolf in sheep's clothing. In Tai Chi it is the power of steel wrapped in cotton. The outer arm stays very relaxed and sensitive while you express the force through the inner arm. Because of this, it is very hard for your opponent to feel your intention through your outer arm, and the power you release from the inner arm is sudden and unexpected.

Press is applied when the opponent tries to tie up your outer arm by trapping it against your body. You move the body back to create more space and then join the back hand to the outer arm and press forward. To uproot your opponent, first apply force in a downward direction to break his root, and then follow with upward force.

Another application of Press is to counter an opponent's Rollback.

PUSH

Although Push looks like applying equal force with both hands, this is not the case. If you were to do that, you would be double-weighted. In Push, you must remember the principles of Yin and Yang. When the weight is on the left leg, the left leg is Yang. Therefore the right hand is your power hand or Yang hand, while the left hand is the Yin, receptive, and sensing hand. Your Yin hand will be feeling for your opponent's weak spot, so your Yang hand will know the most vulnerable place to attack. As you shift the weight forward into the right leg, Yin and Yang suddenly switch; the left hand becomes Yang and the right hand becomes Yin. Therefore if your opponent was mounting resistance against your right hand attack, he may become unbalanced as your right hand suddenly becomes soft and yielding and the anticipated resistance is not there. At that same moment you shift the attack to the left hand and push him away.

Some people think a Push is not a very deadly or effective martial technique, since the opponent isn't hurt and can come right back at you. It is true that a Push can be very gentle and may not hurt the opponent. In many situations, however, it may be all that is needed to cool off a hot-headed attack. When your opponent feels how easily you are able to move her away, yet you do it without injuring her, she may sober up quickly and stop her attack. In this day and age, it is good to know martial techniques that can subdue an opponent without injury. If you don't know how to deal with an aggressor in any way other than kicking and punching, you may escalate a volatile situation unnecessarily.

All that aside, if the situation warrants a more aggressive approach, Push can be a deadly move. A quick Push backed by your whole structure can cause tremendous internal damage to an opponent. The wavelike explosive force of Push can dislocate bones, rupture internal organs, and cause whiplash to the spine. In the case of multiple attackers, you can also use Push to launch one attacker against another, hurl an opponent to the ground, against a wall or tree, or down an incline. Don't underestimate the power of Push!

PULL DOWN

When your opponent punches or pushes straight at you in a horizontal direction, you redirect his force by joining with it and then

steering it suddenly downward. Use your whole body weight to do this with sinking-back energy. This can cause whiplash in your opponent's neck, so be very careful about how much power you use.

SPLIT

Splitting force is used in almost every Tai Chi application. It uses the principle of divide and conquer. In general, when an opponent attacks, you want to divide her force into three directions. Your leg attacks her leg and pushes it in one direction; one of your hands guides her body in a second direction, while the other hand presses her in yet a third direction. Your opponent doesn't know which way to turn and is easily toppled. (See illustrations of Single Whip.)

Another application of Split divides your opponent's force in two. For example, in the sinking back between Press and Push, when your opponent tries to push you with two hands, as you sit back bring the two arms up between your opponent's two arms and expand gently outward like a wedge splitting a log. You can then counter with Push or Press, Elbow Attack, or Shoulder Strike. (See illustrations for Shoulder Strike #2.)

Don't expand too far; you only need to make sure that your opponent's hands clear your body. Anything more is overkill and will give your opponent more opportunity to sense what you are doing and retaliate.

ELBOW ATTACK

If an opponent punches, grab his elbow, fold it, and push it up to send his force back in the reverse direction. When you do this, you can use the opponent's own elbow for leverage to strike his chin, chest, stomach, or rib cage with the point of your elbow. You can also come in with the elbow for a more damaging counter-attack.

There are about 18 different elbow techniques, as well as about the same number of palm techniques. An elbow attack is very powerful, especially when you know how to get your whole body weight and structure behind your elbow. You can break your opponent's rib cage due to the density of the two bones that create the elbow. Again, be careful when you attack with your elbows; you are stronger than you realize.

SHOULDER STRIKE

The shoulder can also be used as an effective weapon against an attack. After a Ward Off, if the back of the opponent's shoulder is exposed, you can cup your own shoulder and launch it out against the opponent. A shoulder strike can either be on the side or in the middle of the opponent.

This type of attack should be done by rounding the scapulae, which prevents the shock of the contact from doing damage to yourself.

Shoulder Strike #1

1. Deflect opponent's attack to the right.
2. Attack his chest with your right shoulder.

This is another reason careful selection of potential attack areas is important.

In particular, if the opponent's arms are up, leaving her sides exposed, a slight sinking motion can allow you to hit your shoulder against the opponent's rib cage or sternum.

Shoulder Strike #2

1. Split your opponents force.
2. Attack his sternum with your shoulder.

Your entire weight is directed from the ground to the hip to the shoulder, which creates a head-on collision between the corner of your shoulder and a vulnerable area on the opponent.

We often fall into the trap of thinking that our hands and feet are our only weapons. In Tai Chi, always remember that the entire body is your weapon. If an opponent grabs your wrist or elbow, relax; let him have your hand while you fold up your arm and attack with your shoulder. A shoulder strike can crack bones, dislocate joints, and knock an opponent unconscious.

SINKING FORCE

Sinking back is very important in providing effective strength to your counterattacks; otherwise it is like pulling the bow back only halfway before releasing an arrow. In Tai Chi, gather your strength within until you have to let it go. The restriction leads to a controlled, directed, and more powerful attack. The entire basis for the sinking force is to connect with the earth to give strength to your attack. Therefore it is important not to bob up and down, or you will be unable to connect with the Earth force.

Partner exercise for Sinking Force training

1. Have your partner push your hips from behind.
2. Sink your weight down into your rear leg and push back with the force of your front leg.

Sinking Force provides the power in Pull Down.

SINGLE WHIP

Single Whip can be viewed as a means of spreading out the forces of an attack from both hands in sequence. At first, the Crane's Beak is used to stick to the wrist of the opponent's first attack (on the same side as the beak). The beak is used to deflect that hand to the side by hooking over from the outside and pulling it out and away.

Next, in the Reaching Up to Heaven motion, the inside of the other wrist deflects the opponent's second attack from the inside, deflecting it out and away. At this point, the opponent is

Single Whip Application

1. Deflect his left punch with Crane's Beak to your right.
2. Deflect his right punch to your left with Reaching to Heaven.

3. Hook his front leg and pull it toward you.
4. Push his chin back with Single Hand Push.

standing with his arms apart, vulnerable to an array of attacks on his midsection.

Single Whip is so named because it can actually be used as a whip. Following a Ward Off, the beak can be whipped into action to "peck" at the opponent's trapezius, for example. This is very painful to the opponent when you can relax and put all your weight and force into the tiny point of the beak. The beak can also be used to go into vulnerable pressure points on the surface of the opponent's body, such as between the joints and vertebrae. The throat center and groin are also lethal areas to attack with the beak.

Cutting Leg

You learn Cutting Leg from the Tai Chi Walk. You may have a chance to cut an opponent's leg because he has to defend all three parts of his body: upper, middle, and lower. This may be beyond his level of awareness. When you do Cutting Leg, your shin needs to be toughened so that you do not cause yourself pain. If you are cutting from the front, it will be shin against shin, and the stronger shin will succeed. For the front Cutting Leg, step behind the foot of the opponent, turn the foot up on the heel, hook around the back of the opponent's leg, and cut down by twisting his ankle with your shin. This can be done from the inside or the outside of the leg.

The masters of Tai Chi use this cutting technique to wage a dual-pronged attack, one above and the other below. Cutting Leg can be

used on virtually every step of attack and counterattack during a confrontation.

Incorporating Applications into the Form

As you practice the Tai Chi form by yourself, you can envision yourself using each of the applications described above in self-defense. This is why Tai Chi is often called "shadow-boxing." This enhances the more practical side

of protecting yourself with Tai Chi, as well as creating an awareness of directing the energy so it will make the moves that much more effective during actual use.

There are many other applications of Tai Chi, which are described in more detail in our forthcoming book, *Tai Chi Chi Kung II.*

16
The Dance of the Tao

Taoism is a way of life that can be expressed through Tai Chi. The Tai Chi practice combines the working growth of body, mind, and energy by finding balance and coordination between these aspects of our being. However, when the practice has ended, the Tao does not stop. The same process of oneness of the body, mind, and energy must continue into daily life.

ONENESS WITH THE TAO

The emphasis in Tai Chi practice is on creating a oneness within oneself, and between oneself and the Tao. This is brought out through a few different levels of practice.

MOVE AS A WHOLE

Moving with the Chi force and allowing it to move with you enables you to absorb and combine the external energy with the life force. At this level, oneness with the Tao starts as one learns to move one's body in an integrated way. Through sensitization, the Chi is brought into harmony with the body.

There is an automatic wholeness to the actions of the lower animals, whereas with people, everything tends to get separated:

hands from legs, mind from body from spirit. This can be seen when people tense their muscles and wind up hurting themselves when they try to lift, pull, or push things. This is because they do not use their bodies in an integrated way. Their mind, hands, legs, and back all work separately, resulting in millions of back injuries, torn knees, and dislocated shoulders each year.

AWARENESS IN MOVEMENT

Awareness in movement is very important in Tai Chi practice. People commonly disassociate their minds and their bodies, often doing one thing while their minds are thinking of something completely different.

In Tai Chi we focus on the most minute details of how we move, breathe, and use our mental intention. With regular practice, this awareness begins to spill over into daily life. Through this increased awareness in practice, the dangers of ordinary life—injuries, mistakes, and accidents—are greatly reduced.

ONENESS WITH NATURE

Division is the sign of the times, whether it be separation by country of origin, cultural heritage, ethnic custom or religion, sex, age, race, or economic status. As a result, we see ourselves as separate from nature and imagine we can despoil the environment without doing any harm to ourselves. We must realize that we can continue to exist only by living in harmony and balance with the universe and with nature.

Bees pollinate as their role in nature, bacteria recycle degradable material, and worms restore the earth for further growth. Without each aspect of nature, only a mountain of death would exist. Everything from trees to stones has its function in nature, and yet we allow ourselves to become alienated from the ground of our own being.

The movement of the Tao is a continuous flow from Yin to Yang; the day flows into the night, the sun cycles with the moon, and the winter yields to the summer. All these aspects of nature participate in an endless cycle, keeping the universe in balance. This we can experience through the practice of Tai Chi.

The Tao

The Tao is more than just a philosophy or an intellectual exercise. It is truly a whole way of living, through which the various levels of practice, if fully implemented, can provide enjoyment, happiness, and fulfillment.

The Tao is the way of living in harmony with nature and the universe that has guided Chinese civilization for five thousand years. But the only way to realize practical benefits from the Tao is to cultivate and practice it. To put it simply, "If you do it, you get it; if you don't do it, you don't get it!"

Tai Chi Chi Kung is an integral part of the Tao, the dance of Yin and Yang. All the principles of the Tao are within Tai Chi Chi Kung practice. Practice daily, and you yourself will gradually become an embodiment of the Tao. Balance, harmony, and integrity will be present in everything you do; you will begin to move through life with Wu Wei, effortlessness, not doing yet leaving nothing undone.

APPENDIX 1
Energetic Preparations for Tai Chi Chi Kung

THE INNER SMILE

The Inner Smile is a powerful relaxation and self-healing technique that uses the energy of happiness and love as a language to communicate with the internal organs of the body. A genuine smile transmits loving energy that has the power to calm, balance, and heal.

If you learn to smile inwardly to the organs and glands, your whole body will feel loved and appreciated. The Inner Smile begins at the eyes and mid-eyebrow point. The eyes are connected to the autonomic nervous system, which in turn is connected to all the muscles, organs, and glands.

As one of the first parts of the body to receive signals, the eyes cause the organs and glands to accelerate activity at times of stress or danger, and to slow down when a crisis has passed. When the eyes relax, they activate the parasympathetic nervous system and cause the rest of the body to relax.

As you activate the loving energy, you will feel the energy of the Inner Smile flow down the entire length of the body like a waterfall. This is a very powerful and effective tool to counteract stress and tension.

How to Do the Inner Smile

There are three vital parts to each phase of the Inner Smile. First, direct the awareness to a specific part of the body. Second, smile to that part of the body; send it a genuine feeling of love, gratitude, and appreciation for its role in keeping the body running smoothly and in good health. Third, feel that part of the body relax and smile back to you.

1. Stand in Wu Chi Stance (see chapter 5) or sit on the edge of a chair with the hands comfortably clasped together and resting on the lap. Keep the eyes closed and breathe normally. Follow the breathing until it becomes smooth, quiet, deep, even, calm, and soft.

2. Relax the forehead. Imagine yourself in one of your favorite beautiful places in the world. Recall the sights, sounds, and sensations of that place until they are vividly in your mind's eye. Then imagine suddenly meeting someone you love. Picture him or her smiling lovingly and radiantly at you. Feel yourself basking in the warmth of that smile like sunshine, drawing it into your eyes. Feel the eyes

relaxing and responding with a smile of their own.

3. Picture the healing Chi of nature—the fresh energy of waterfalls, mountains, and oceans—as a golden cloud of benevolent loving energy in front of you. We call this the Higher Human Plane energy of the atmosphere, the blended Chi of Heaven and Earth, or the Cosmic Particle force. Direct the smiling energy in the eyes to this Cosmic Particle energy around you, drawing it into the mid-eyebrow point. Feel the brow relaxing and widening. Spiral the energy into the mid-eyebrow point; feel it amplifying the power of your smile.

4. Let the smiling awareness flow down over the cheeks, down through the jaw muscles and tongue, and down through the neck and throat, soothing and relaxing as it goes.

5. Smile down to the thymus gland and heart. Feel them open like flowers in the morning with love, joy, and happiness bubbling out of them.

6. Smile down to the rest of the solid organs: lungs, liver, pancreas, spleen, kidneys, sexual organs, and reproductive system. Thank each of them for their work in keeping you vibrant and healthy.

This completes the First Line of the Inner Smile.

7. Return the awareness to the eyes, and recharge the energy of your smile. Then draw in more of the golden light of the Cosmic Particle force.

8. Roll the tongue around the mouth until you have gathered some saliva. Smile to the saliva and draw the smiling energy and the golden light into the saliva, transforming it into a healing nectar.

9. Swallow the saliva in two or three strong gulps. Follow it with awareness down the esophagus, smiling as it goes, feeling the healing nectar soothing and refreshing the esophagus. Continue smiling through the rest of the digestive tract: the stomach, small intestine, gall bladder, large intestine, rectum, anus, bladder, and ure-thra. Thank these organs for their work in giving you energy through ingestion, digestion, absorption, and elimination.

This completes the Second or Middle Line of the Inner Smile.

10. Return the awareness to the eyes, and recharge your smile. Then once again connect with the golden light of the Cosmic Particle force.

11. Smile to the brain, to the left and right hemispheres, and to the pituitary, thalamus, and pineal glands. Then smile down through the spinal column vertebra by vertebra, thanking each vertebra for its work in protecting the spinal cord and supporting the skeletal structure. This completes the Third or Back Line of the Inner Smile.

12. Return the awareness to the eyes once again and recharge your smiling energy.

13. Smile down through the whole body, particularly to any place that feels tired, sore, painful, weak, empty, or tense. Shower these parts with the healing nectar of your smiling awareness.

14. Finally, smile to the navel and collect the energy there.

Men: Starting in the center of the navel, spiral the energy outward in a clockwise direction, making 36 revolutions. Take care not to make the outer ring of the spiral any larger than a grapefruit; circling above the diaphragm causes too much energy to flow into the heart and over-stimulates the emotions, whereas circling below the pubic bone sends too much energy into the reproductive system, where it may be lost through ejaculation (or menses, for women).

When you have completed the clockwise revolutions, spiral inward in the opposite direction 24 times, ending at the center of the navel.

Women: Spiral the energy similarly to the way described for men, but begin spiraling outward from the navel in a counter-clockwise direction and spiral back inward in a clockwise direction.

THE MICROCOSMIC ORBIT MEDITATION

The Microcosmic Orbit meditation awakens, circulates, and directs Chi through the Governor Channel, which ascends from the base of the spine to the crown, and the Functional Channel (also called the Conception Vessel), which runs down the front midline. Dedicated practice of this ancient esoteric method eliminates stress and nervous tension, energizes the internal organs, restores health to damaged tissues, and establishes a peaceful sense of well-being.

The meditations of the Microcosmic Orbit system also strengthen the Original Chi and teach you the basics of circulating Chi. They allow the palms, the soles of the feet, the mid-eyebrow point, and the crown to open. These specific locations are the major points at which energy can be absorbed, condensed, and transformed into fresh new life force.

How to Practice the Basic Microcosmic Orbit Meditation

The Tai Chi Classics say, "The mind moves and the Chi follows." Therefore, when you focus the attention at a specific place in the body, you automatically activate the Chi at that place. By the mere act of attention, you consciously link the brain to the local sensory receptors at that place. The nervous system in turn creates local changes in capillary circulation, muscle activity, and lymphatic flow.

All the movements in these systems require energy; we call this energy Chi. The sensations of these energetic changes can be subtle or dramatic. They are characterized by such feelings as warmth, tingling, pulsing, expansion, vibration, or effervescence. You may sense one or more of these feelings depending on your sensitivity and experience with meditation and Chi Kung. Don't worry if you feel little or nothing at first; just focus the attention at each point, and whether you feel it or not, your Chi will be moving.

With practice, you will begin to feel the Chi moving more vividly.

1. **Begin with the Inner Smile.** As you did for the Inner Smile, stand in Wu Chi Stance (see chapter 5) or sit on the edge of a chair with the hands comfortably clasped together and resting on the lap. Keep the eyes closed and breathe normally. Follow the breathing until it becomes smooth, quiet, deep, even, calm, and soft.

   Smile down to the front, middle, and back lines to relax and harmonize the body, breath, and mind. At the end, smile to the lower Tan Tien, but do not collect energy yet.

2. **Activate the Original Chi in the lower Tan Tien.** Focus the attention on the lower Tan Tien, breathing naturally using lower abdominal breathing. Use the intention to create a feeling of warmth in the lower Tan Tien. Feel it as the reservoir of your Original Chi, the main battery of your entire energetic system. Imagine that each breath is like a bellows, fanning the fire in the lower Tan Tien. Hold the awareness there until you feel the lower Tan Tien is filled with Chi.

3. **Begin to move the energy in the Functional Channel.** Move the awareness to the navel and concentrate there until you feel the energy has gathered at that point. Then bring the attention to the sexual center (Sperm/Ovary Palace). When you feel sufficient energy gathered there, proceed in a similar way to the perineum (Gate of Life and Death).

4. **Direct the energy through the Governor Channel.** When you have accumulated substantial energy at each point, move the awareness to the next successive point. From the perineum, continue concentrating the energy at each point up the spine to the head: to the coccyx, sacral hiatus, Door of Life, T-11, Jade Pillow, Crown, and mid-eyebrow point (Third Eye).

5. **Connect the two channels.** Bring the attention to the tip of the tongue. Touch the tip of the tongue to the palate, connecting the two main channels of the Microcosmic Orbit. Press and release the tongue against the palate 9 to 36 times. This activates the palate point and

enables the energy to flow down the Functional Channel.

6. **Complete the circulation in the Functional Channel.** Direct the attention to each point along the Functional Channel: to the Throat center, Heart center, solar plexus, and back to the navel. This completes one cycle of the Microcosmic Orbit. You may notice less sensation in the Functional Channel because there are seven parallel pathways along which the energy may descend, and thus the energy may become more diffuse.

7. **Continue to circulate the Microcosmic Orbit.** Circulate the energy through the entire cycle at least 9 to 10 times. As you gain experience, you can increase the number of circulations to 36, 72, 108, or 360.

At some point you may feel the energy begin to move by itself. This is a good sign; if it happens, don't try to restrain it, just let it flow at its own pace.

Connect to the Chi of Heaven, Earth and Man

1. Once you have opened the Microcosmic Orbit, open the soles of the feet to the earth and allow the Earth energy to ascend the legs to the perineum to join the Microcosmic Orbit. You may perceive this energy as a cool blue light with the mind's eye.

2. When the energy reaches the top of the head, open the Crown point to receive the Heavenly force and join it with the Microcosmic Orbit. You may experience this as a warm violet light coming from the North Star.

3. When the energy reaches the mid-eyebrow point, relax the brow and reconnect with the Cosmic Particle force you experienced during the Inner Smile. Allow this golden light to join with the Microcosmic Orbit.

4. When you are finished, guide the energy back to the navel and collect it by spiraling it 36 times outward and 24 times inward, as at the end of the Inner Smile.

Spend at least one to two weeks concentrating on completing the Microcosmic Orbit before proceeding to learn the Tai Chi Chi Kung form. Read through the book *Awaken Healing Energy Through the Tao* or *Awaken Healing Light of the Tao*, especially the question-and-answer sections. This material will help you tremendously throughout your whole life.

For Those Having Difficulty Completing the Microcosmic Orbit

It takes some people longer than others to complete the Microcosmic Orbit, depending on their level of energy, state of general health, number of obstructions in the channels, and how long it takes to clear each obstruction.

1. If after two weeks you have not completed the entire Microcosmic Orbit successfully, reverse the energy flow one center at a time, starting from the last point you have reached.

2. Spend more time at the Door of Life.

3. Then bring the energy down to the perineum and down the backs of the legs to the Kidney points at the soles of the feet.

4. Then, proceeding up along the inner sides of the legs, return to the perineum.

5. Then continue up to the sexual center, then to the navel, and then up to the solar plexus. Spend one week concentrating on the solar plexus point.

6. Then proceed to the Heart point and spend one week concentrating there.

7. Then advance to the Throat point and spend one week there.

This procedure will open up the Functional Channel. Once you have opened the Functional Channel, bring the energy to the tip of the tongue, thereby connecting this route with the Governor Channel. Your Microcosmic Orbit should now be running properly. If not, concentrate on any points along the spine that feel obstructed for one week at each point, and you should be assured of success.

IRON SHIRT CHI KUNG STANDING MEDITATION

Iron Shirt Chi Kung is one of the martial arts aspects of the Healing Tao system,. It is also an important foundation for both healing and spiritual work. Iron Shirt Chi Kung develops internal power and a well-conditioned body through simple techniques that build and store Chi. These techniques also help you become rooted to the earth's energy, which keeps the body centered and balanced.

There are many aspects to Iron Shirt Chi Kung training. Here we present only the basics needed in your practice of Tai Chi Chi Kung.

To fully master Iron Shirt, you must study personally with a qualified instructor. You may also refer to the books *Iron Shirt Chi Kung* and *Bone Marrow Nei Kung*.

Basic Iron Shirt Chi Kung: Embracing the Tree

1. Stand with the feet parallel, knee-to-toe-length apart. Bend the knees slightly as if crouching. Gently twist the legs outward as though they were screwing into the ground. Tilt the sacrum and tailbone forward until you feel the feet press firmly into the ground. Round the scapulae, relax the chest, and hold the head erect. Position the arms as if they were encircling a tree, keeping the elbows sunk. Point the thumbs upward, point the rest of the fingers toward the corresponding fingers on the other hand, and gently stretch the fingers apart until the tendons have become taut but not tense. Keep the weight balanced over the Bubbling Spring point of the feet. Feel the whole skeletal structure in perfect alignment with gravity.

2. Allow the body to rock slightly forward and back and side to side to open to the Earth energy rising up.

3. Practice Bellows Breathing: as you inhale, press the diaphragm down and expand the lower abdomen, sides, and back at waist level. As you exhale, raise the diaphragm and pull the stomach in. Take about one second for each complete breath (in and out). Repeat 18-36 times.

4. Practice all the stages of the Microcosmic Orbit in this position. If the arms feel tired, lower them but maintain the circle structure of the arms.

5. Practice Bone Breathing and Marrow Washing (described later in this book).

6. Conclude by collecting energy at the navel.

APPENDIX 2
Tai Chi Physiology
by Albert L. Chan, Ph.D.

The ancient Chinese martial art of Tai Chi was developed through years of experience and practice. In the West, however, with the advances of science, many question the basis for the vast increase in power that can be achieved through the practice. In response to those who insist, "Show me, I'm from Missouri," we include the beginnings of a scientific investigation that has been provided by Albert L. Chan, Ph.D.

THE INNER STRUCTURE

The human skeleton, viewed as a system, is effectively a biomechanical power transporter. Mechanical power can be transferred from one end of the system to the other only provided that all the involved components are in proper alignment (which is why structure is so important). Tai Chi has developed from the study of the coordination and structure of movement, such that the power from the legs can be transported to the pelvis, to the base of the spine, to each vertebra of the spine, to the scapulae, and ultimately through the forearms and hands, its destination in self-defense. Poor posture or improper alignment restricts the flow of this power.

Because the legs, which generate the power, have the strongest and largest muscles in the human body, the force they can transmit to the attacking arm is tremendous. This force can be used to throw opponents many feet away or to incapacitate an opponent by exerting a powerful push or punch.

The Tai Chi form evolved as a way in which energy from specific power points in the body could be directed and focused through the use of structure. By carefully training each part of the body to perform only a few functions, the techniques that were developed are relatively easy to master.

The forward and backward directions of motion and balance are controlled by both legs, since they are the power source. The hips control the rotational motion of the entire upper torso, as well as the legs. This force plays a particularly important role in using this circular action to redirect an opponent's attack. When a direct force is encountered, rather then requiring the power to both overcome and redirect the force, the circular action uses the oncoming power of the attack and follows it through by deflecting it away from the body.

The spine transfers the power from the hips to the scapulae through its ability to twist and flex in a controlled and supple way. An unnaturally twisted or curved spine reduces the amount of power that can be transferred. The scapulae control the flow of this power and the movement of both arms through a careful positioning relative to the spine. When the hips, spine, and scapulae move as one unit, an integrated strength is created that is more powerful than any of its individual components.

The arms are used to feel the approaching force of the opponent and to begin the process of partially receiving and partially deflecting this power accordingly.

All the parts of the body should be relaxed so that the oncoming force can be sensed and reacted to without resistance. A tensed arm or shoulder increases reaction time and simultaneously reduces the efficient transfer of power through the body, thus allowing lessof the oncoming force to flow through the structure. On the other hand, a relaxed body produces an increase in the amount of power being generated.

A good example of this is a simple push. The structure collects power from the legs as they are pressing into the ground, from the hips as they rotate, from the spine as it flexes, and from the shoulders as they extend. At each point, the total power increases as it is directed up the body to the attacking arm or shoulder. The amount of power that reaches the pushing hand or fist is much greater than that which is being produced just at the legs.

The structure is also used as a lever to deflect or diverge an opponent's powerful blow or push. A powerful oncoming push can either be redirected to another direction (deflection) or absorbed to a great extent by the structure through the spine and down the legs,where it diverges into the ground, leaving the practitioner unharmed. This is the essence of rooting. The proper alignment of the structure of the body provides a path for this great power to flow through, while providing additional energy to other points of the body for a counterattack.

The Tai Chi Chi Kung Form

There are eight basic movements in Tai Chi: Ward Off, Roll Back, Press, Push, Pull Down, Split, Elbow Strike, and Shoulder Strike. When the basic principles are understood and applied, the practitioner can employ other equally effective techniques.

Tai Chi uses gravity and the leverage of the legs for pulling the opponent off balance. An important aspect of the practice is avoiding moving one's center of gravity up and down, which would waste a considerable amount of energy as well as interfering with a smooth structural motion.

The structure of the person acts like a rubber ball. The harder you strike it, the more it yields (sinking) and the more force it returns to the opponent by bouncing back. Ultimately, the ball has the advantage, because the attacker becomes exhausted as his attacking force is absorbed.

The Tendons

Holding correct Tai Chi posture implies using the minimal amount of energy to withstand the maximum oncoming force. Furthermore, a good posture in Tai Chi uses the tendons instead of the muscles for proper rooting and power.

In a Roll Back movement to the left, as the practitioner turns the hip to the left, the left thigh is being led in the same direction. Since the left foot is stationary on the ground, and the knee is virtually a hinge joint (cannot be twisted rotationally), the length of the left leg is twisted, which in turn wraps the leg tendons around the bones. As a result, these tendons are stretched.

The tendons are flexible and elastic. As a result, they can store energy by stretching and winding like a rubber band. The Achilles tendons in particular, which are located at the ankles, are the largest tendons in the human body and are capable of storing the energy of a 1,000-pound pull. The Roll Back to the left stores a considerable amount of energy in the left leg tendons. The stored energy is then released back to the body as the left leg unwinds and turns the body into the Press posture. The energy is thus stored or gathered in the Roll Back and released in the Press. This is true of almost all the Yin-to-Yang transitions in the Tai Chi form.

The tendons act like springs. A correct posture can absorb and redirect force like a spring in a car's suspension. In a sense, the tendons conserve and recycle energy that would otherwise be wasted.

A similar technique is used by a baseball pitcher, who winds up his body and hips to the extreme before throwing the baseball. Likewise, in most other martial arts, prior to throwing the kick or punch, the body is fully torqued. However, with Tai Chi, the key advantage is through the extensive use of tendon power.

This use of tendon power can be found throughout the Tai Chi form. For instance, in the right-hand Single Whip movement, the standing leg (right) is twisted approximately 40 degrees or more with the foot remaining flat and stationary on the ground. Energy is stored in the leg tendons, which is then released to help the body unwind and execute the strike with the right hand by extending the beak.

To illustrate the point, one can hold the right-hand Single Whip posture and not perform the strike. If the practitioner then lifts up the left leg so that it does not touch the ground, the right leg naturally unwinds and releases the stored energy to turn the body to the left.

The tendons are also used to absorb and rebound back the power from an opponent's push. When a practitioner is being pushed at the hands while in a Press posture, the force travels from the hand to the elbow, and part of that energy is used to stretch the triceps tendon. The rest of the force travels to the shoulders, which also consume part of the energy through the tendons around the scapulae. As the residual force is transmitted down the spine and to the back of the leg, energy is absorbed along the tendons that help support these areas. All excess force is then transmitted into the ground through the nine points of the feet. When the opponent's power has been absorbed in this manner, the practitioner can release this stored energy along with his or her own additional muscle power, yielding a much more powerful counter. A returned Press can either throw the opponent off balance or lift him up and project him several feet away.

Research

In recent research on runners, it has been confirmed that leg tendons (especially the Achilles tendons) increase the efficiency of running. Tendons absorb the energy of landing and release it for the subsequent push from the ground. If the tendons were not elastic, the runner would require three times the energy to run the same distance.

This effect is more apparent on four-legged animals such as horses or camels. Their lower legs consist mainly of tendons, which maximize the efficiency of running and conserving energy.

Furthermore, the author has proven (in a doctoral dissertation) that hand tendons increase the maximum speed of a forward punch, because of their elasticity, by as much as 6 percent, which is equivalent to a 12 percent increase in impact power.

Conclusions

Tai Chi uses correct posture to distribute energy to the entire body, to redirect force, and to pass force to the ground. On demand, the structure collects energy from the tendons and muscles and focuses it to a point for striking.

Besides the awesome power that Tai Chi can control, it promotes good physical health because of the exercise provided to the spine, hips, legs, and arms and their associated tendons, muscles, and joints. It also trains the mind to develop a vital life force (called Chi) within the body. The physical and mental exercise enhance each other to bring long life to the practitioner.

Tai Chi is an art that applies the fundamentals of movement and body structure. Tai Chi focuses and channels power within the body for the purpose of self-defense, which is then expressed optimally in terms of the efficient use of energy.

Albert L. Chan has practiced and studied Tai Chi Chi Kung and Taoist Meditation for 14 years with

Master Chia. He has also studied Wing Tsun Chuan for 12 years. He holds a Ph.D. degree in physics and a Masters degree in computer science. Currently, Dr. Chan is doing research on the physics of sport. He is particularly interested in analyzing the martial arts and sports.

Bibliography

Chia, Mantak and Maneewan.
Awaken Healing Light of the Tao
Huntington, NY: Healing Tao Books, 1993.

Chia, Mantak, and Michael Winn.
Taoist Secrets of Love:
Cultivating Male Sexual Energy.
Santa Fe, NM: Aurora Press, 1984.

Chia, Mantak.
Taoist Ways to Transform Stress into Vitality.
Huntington, NY: Healing Tao Books, 1985.

Chia, Mantak and Maneewan.
Iron Shirt Chi Kung I.
Huntington, NY: Healing Tao Books, 1986.

Chia, Mantak and Maneewan.
Bone Marrow Nei Kung.
Huntington, NY: Healing Tao Books, 1989.

Chia, Mantak and Maneewan.
Fusion of the Five Elements I.
Huntington, NY: Healing Tao Books, 1989.

Chia, Mantak and Maneewan.
Chi Nei Tsang: Internal Organs Chi Massage.
Huntington, NY: Healing Tao Books, 1990.

Cleary, Thomas, trans.
The Taoist I Ching.
Boston: Shambhala, 1986.

Horwitz, Tem and Susan Kimmelman with
H.H. Lui.
T'ai Chi Ch'uan: The Technique of Power.
Chicago: Chicago Review Press, 1976.

Lee, Ying-Arng.
Lee's Modified Tai Chi Chuan for Health.
Hong Kong: Unicorn Press, 1968.

Liao, Waysun.
Tai Chi Classics.
Boston & London: Shambhala, 1990.

Lo, Benjamin Pang Jeng, with Martin Inn,
Robert Amacker and Susan Foe (translators
and editors).
The Essence of T'ai Chi Ch'uan:
The Literary Tradition.
Richmond, CA: North Atlantic Books, 1979.

Jou, Tsung Hwa.
The Tao of Tai-Chi Chuan.
Rutland, VT: Charles E. Tuttle Co., 1980.

Olson, Stuart Alve (compiler) and Gerald Kuehl (editor).
Imagination Becomes Reality:
The Teachings of Master T. T. Liang.
St. Cloud, MN: Bubbling Well Press, 1986.

Wang Peisheng & Zeng Weiqi.
Wu Style Taijiquan.
Hong Kong: Hai Feng Publishing Company, 1983.

The International Tao Healing System

THE GOAL OF THE TAOIST PRACTICE

The Healing Tao is a practical system of self-development that enables the individual to complete the harmonious evolution of the physical, mental, and spiritual planes the achievement of spiritual independence.

Through a series of ancient Chinese meditative and internal energy exercises, the practitioner learns to increase physical energy, release tension, improve health, practice self-defense, and gain the ability to heal oneself and others. In the process of creating a solid foundation of health and well-being in the physical body, the basis for developing one's spiritual independence is also created. While learning to tap the natural energies of the Sun, Moon, Earth, and Stars, a level of awareness is attained in which a solid spiritual body is developed and nurtured.

The ultimate goal of the Tao practice is the transcendence of physical boundaries through the development of the soul and the spirit within man.

International Healing Tao Course Offerings

There are now many International Healing Tao centers in the United States, Canada, Bermuda, Germany, Netherlands, Switzerland, Austria, France, Spain, India, Japan, and Australia offering personal instruction in various practices including the Microcosmic Orbit, the Healing Love Meditation, Tai Chi Chi Kung, Iron Shirt Chi Kung, and the Fusion Meditations.

Healing Tao Warm Current Meditation, as these practices are also known, awakens, circulates, directs, and preserves the generative life-force called Chi through the major acupuncture meridians of the body. Dedicated practice of this ancient, esoteric system eliminates stress and nervous tension, massages the internal organs, and restores health to damaged tissues.

Outline of the Complete System of The Healing Tao

Courses are taught at our various centers. Direct all written inquiries to one central address or call:

The Healing Tao Center
1205 O'Neill Highway
Dunmore, PA 18512
717-348-4310 • Fax 717-348-4313

INTRODUCTORY LEVEL I:
Awaken Your Healing Light

Course 1: (1) *Opening of the Microcosmic Channel;* (2) *The Inner Smile;* (3) *The Six Healing Sounds;* and (4) *Tao Rejuvenation – Chi Self-Massage.*

INTRODUCTORY LEVEL II:
Development of Internal Power

Course 2: *Healing Love:* Seminal and Ovarian Kung Fu.

Course 3: *Iron Shirt Chi Kung:* Organs Exercise and Preliminary Rooting Principle. The Iron Shirt practice is divided into three workshops: Iron Shirt I, II, and III.

Course 4: *Fusion of the Five Elements; Cleansing and Purifying the Organs, and Opening of the Six Special Channels.* The Fusion practice is divided into three workshops: Fusion I, II, and III.

Course 5: *Tai Chi Chi Kung; the Foundation of Tai Chi Chuan.* The Tai Chi practice is divided into seven workshops: (1) Original Thirteen Movements' Form (five directions, eight movements); (2) Fast Form of Discharging Energy; (3) Long Form (108 movements); (4) Tai Chi Sword; (5) Tai Chi Knife; (6) Tai Chi Short and Long Stick; (7) Self-Defense Applications and Mat Work.

Course 6: *Taoist Five Element Nutrition; Taoist Healing Diet.*

INTRODUCTORY LEVEL III:
The Way of Radiant Health

Course 7: *Healing Hands Kung Fu; Awaken the Healing Hand – Five Finger Kung Fu.*

Course 8: *Chi Nei Tsang; Organ Chi Transformation Massage.* This practice is divided into three levels: Chi Nei Tsang I, II, and III.

Course 9: *Space Dynamics; The Taoist Art of Energy Placement.*

INTERMEDIATE LEVEL:
Foundations of Spiritual Practice

Course 10: *Lesser Enlightenment Kan and Li:* Opening of the Twelve Channels; Raising the Soul, and Developing the Energy Body.

Course 11: *Greater Enlightenment Kan and Li:* Raising the Spirit and Developing the Spiritual Body.

Course 12: *Greatest Enlightenment:* Educating the Spirit and the Soul; Space Travel.

ADVANCED LEVEL:
The Immortal Tao The Realm of Soul and Spirit

Course 13: *Sealing of the Five Senses.*

Course 14: *Congress of Heaven and Earth.*

Course 15: *Reunion of Heaven and Man.*

Course Descriptions of The Healing Tao System

INTRODUCTORY LEVEL I:
Awaken Your Healing Light

A. The first level of the Healing Tao system involves opening the Microcosmic Orbit within yourself. An open Microcosmic Orbit enables you to expand outward to connect with the Universal, Cosmic Particle, and Earth Forces. Their combined forces are considered by Taoists as the Light of Warm Current Meditation.

Through unique relaxation and concentration techniques, this practice awakens, circulates, directs, and preserves the generative life-force, or Chi, through the first two major acupuncture channels (or meridians) of the body: the Functional Channel which runs down the chest, and the Governor Channel which ascends the middle of the back.

Dedicated practice of this ancient, esoteric method eliminates stress and nervous tension, massages the internal organs, restores health to damaged tissues, increases the consciousness of being alive, and establishes a sense of well-being. Master Chia and certified instructors will assist students in opening the Microcosmic Orbit by passing energy through their hands or eyes into the students' energy channels.

B. The Inner Smile is a powerful relaxation technique that utilizes the expanding energy of happiness as a language with which to communicate with the internal organs of the body. By learning to smile inwardly to the organs and glands, the whole body will feel loved and appreciated. Stress and tension will be counteracted, and the flow of Chi increased. One feels the energy descend down the entire length of the body like a waterfall. The Inner Smile will help the student to counteract stress, and help to direct and increase the flow of Chi.

C. The Six Healing Sounds is a basic relaxation technique utilizing simple arm movements and special sounds to produce a cooling effect upon the internal organs. These special sounds vibrate specific organs, while the arm movements, combined with posture, guide heat and pressure out of the body. The results are improved digestion, reduced internal stress, reduced insomnia and headaches, and greater vitality as the Chi flow increases through the different organs.

The Six Healing Sounds method is beneficial to anyone practicing various forms of meditation, martial arts, or sports in which there is a tendency to build up excessive heat in the system.

D. Taoist Rejuvenation—Chi Self-Massage is a method of hands-on self-healing work using one's internal energy, or Chi, to strengthen and rejuvenate the sense organs (eyes, ears, nose, tongue), teeth, skin, and inner organs. Using internal power (Chi) and gentle external stimulation, this simple, yet highly effective, self-massage technique enables one to dissolve some of the energy blocks and stress points responsible for disease and the aging process. Taoist Rejuvenation dates back 5000 years to the Yellow Emperor's classic text on Taoist internal medicine.

Completion of the Microcosmic Orbit, the Inner Smile, the Six Healing Sounds, and Tao Rejuvenation techniques are prerequisites for any student who intends to study Introductory Level II of the Healing Tao practice.

INTRODUCTORY LEVEL II:
Development of Internal Power

Course 2: *Healing Love:* Seminal and Ovarian Kung Fu; Transforming Sexual Energy to Higher Centers, and the Art of Harmonious Relationships.

For more than five thousand years of Chinese history, the "no-outlet method" of retaining the seminal fluid during sexual union has remained a well-guarded secret. At first it was practiced exclusively by the Emperor and his innermost circle. Then, it passed from father to chosen son alone, excluding all female family members. Seminal and Ovarian Kung Fu practices teach men and women how to transform and circulate sexual energy through the Microcosmic Orbit. Rather than eliminating sexual intercourse, ancient Taoist yogis learned how to utilize sexual energy as a means of enhancing their internal practice.

The conservation and transformation of sexual energy during intercourse acts as a revitalizing factor in the physical and spiritual development of both men and women. The turning back and circulating of the generative force from the sexual organs to the higher energy centers of the body invigorates and rejuvenates all the vital functions. Mastering this practice produces a deep sense of respect for all forms of life.

In ordinary sexual union, the partners usually experience a type of orgasm which is limited to the genital area. Through special Taoist techniques, men and women learn to experience a total body orgasm without indiscriminate loss of vital energy. The conservation and transformation of sexual energy is essential for the work required in advanced Taoist practice.

Seminal and Ovarian Kung Fu is one of the five main branches of Taoist Esoteric Yoga.

Course 3: *Iron Shirt Chi Kung; Organs Exercises and Preliminary Rooting Principle.*

The Iron Shirt practice is divided into three parts: Iron Shirt I, II, and III.

The physical integrity of the body is sustained and protected through the accumulation and circulation of internal power (Chi) in the vital organs. The Chi energy that began to circulate freely through the Microcosmic Orbit and later the Fusion practices can be stored in the fasciae as well as in the vital organs. Fasciae are layers of connective tissues covering, supporting, or connecting the organs and muscles.

The purpose of storing Chi in the organs and muscles is to create a protective layer of interior power that enables the body to withstand unexpected injuries. Iron Shirt training roots the body to the Earth, strengthens the vital organs, changes the tendons, cleanses the bone marrow, and creates a reserve of pure Chi energy.

Iron Shirt Chi Kung is one of the foundations of spiritual practices since it provides a firm rooting for the ascension of the spirit body. The higher the spirit goes, the more solid its rooting to the Earth must be.

Iron Shirt Chi Kung I - **Connective Tissues' and Organs' Exercise:**

On the first level of Iron Shirt, by using certain standing postures, muscle locks, and Iron Shirt Chi Kung breathing techniques, one learns how to draw and circulate energy from the ground. The standing postures teach how to connect the internal structure (bones, muscles, tendons, and fasciae) with the ground so that rooting power is developed. Through breathing techniques, internal power is directed to the organs, the twelve tendon channels, and the fasciae.

Over time, Iron Shirt strengthens the vital organs as well as the tendons, muscles, bones, and marrow. As the internal structure is strengthened through layers of Chi energy, the problems of poor posture and circulation of energy are corrected. The practitioner learns the importance of being physically and psychologically rooted in the Earth, a vital factor in the more advanced stages of Taoist practice.

Iron Shirt Chi Kung II - **Tendons' Exercise:**

In the second level of Iron Shirt, one learns how to combine the mind, heart, bone structure, and Chi flow into one moving unit. The static forms learned in the first level of Iron Shirt evolve at this level into moving postures. The goal of Iron Shirt II is to develop rooting power and the ability to absorb and discharge energy through the tendons. A series of exercises allow the student to change, grow, and strengthen the tendons, to stimulate the vital organs, and to integrate the fasciae, tendons, bones, and muscles into one piece. The student also learns methods for releasing accumulated toxins in the muscles and joints of the body. Once energy flows freely through the organs, accumulated poisons can be discharged out of the body very efficiently without resorting to extreme fasts or special dietary aids.

Iron Shirt Chi Kung I is a prerequisite for this course.

Bone Marrow Nei Kung (Iron Shirt Chi Kung III) – Cleansing the Marrow:

In the third level of Iron Shirt, one learns how to cleanse and grow the bone marrow, regenerate sexual hormones and store them in the fasciae, tendons, and marrow, as well as how to direct the internal power to the higher energy centers.

This level of Iron Shirt works directly on the organs, bones, and tendons in order to strengthen the entire system beyond its ordinary capacity. An extremely efficient method of vibrating the internal organs allows the practitioner to shake toxic deposits out of the inner structure of each organ by enhancing Chi circulation. This once highly secret method of advanced Iron Shirt, also known as the Golden Bell System, draws the energy produced in the sexual organs into the higher energy centers to carry out advanced Taoist practices.

Iron Shirt Chi Kung is one of the five essential branches of Taoist Esoteric Practice.

Prior study of Iron Shirt Chi Kung I and Healing Love are prerequisites for this course.

Course 4: *Fusion of the Five Elements, Cleansing of the Organs, and Opening of the Six Special Channels.*

Fusion of the Five Elements and Cleansing of the Organs I, II, and III is the second formula of the Taoist Yoga Meditation of Internal Alchemy. At this level, one learns how the five elements (Earth, Metal, Fire, Wood, and Water), and their corresponding organs (spleen, lungs, heart, liver, and kidneys) interact with one another in three distinct ways: producing, combining, and strengthening. The Fusion practice combines the energies of the five elements and their corresponding emotions into one harmonious whole.

Fusion of the Five Elements I:

In this practice of internal alchemy, the student learns to transform the negative emotions of worry, sadness, cruelty, anger, and fear into pure energy. This process is accomplished by identifying the source of the negative emotions within the five organs of the body. After the excessive energy of the emotions is filtered out of the organs, the state of psycho/physical balance is restored to the body. Freed of negative emotions, the pure energy of the five organs is crystallized into a radiant pearl or crystal ball. The pearl is circulated in the body and attracts to it energy from external sources—Universal Energy, Cosmic Particle Energy, and Earth Energy. The pearl plays a central role in the development and nourishment of the soul or energy body. The energy body then is nourished with the pure (virtue) energy of the five organs.

Fusion of the Five Elements II:

The second level of Fusion practice teaches additional methods of circulating the pure energy of the five organs once they are freed of negative emotions. When the five organs are cleansed, the positive emotions of kindness, gentleness, respect, fairness, justice, and compassion rise as a natural expression of internal balance. The practitioner is able to monitor his state of balance by observing the quality of emotions arising spontaneously within.

The energy of the positive emotions is used to open the three channels running from the perineum, at the base of the sexual organs, to the top of the head. These channels collectively are known as the Thrusting Channels or Routes. In addition, a series of nine levels called the Belt Channel is opened, encircling the nine major energy centers of the body.

Fusion of Five Elements III:

The third level of Fusion practice completes the cleansing of the energy channels in the body by opening the positive and negative leg and arm channels. The opening of the Microcosmic Orbit, the Thrusting Channels, the Belt Channel, the Great Regulator, and Great Bridge Channels makes the body extremely permeable to the circulation of vital energy. The unhindered circulation of energy is the foundation of perfect physical and emotional health.

The Fusion practice is one of the greatest achievements of the ancient Taoist masters, as it gives the individual a way of freeing the body of negative emotions, and, at the same time, allows the pure virtues to shine forth.

Course 5: *Tai Chi Chi Kung;*
The Foundation of Tai Chi Chuan.

The Tai Chi practice is divided into seven workshops: (1) the Original Thirteen Movements' Form (five directions, eight movements); (2) Fast Form of Discharging Energy; (3) Long Form (108 movements); (4) Tai Chi Sword; (5) Tai Chi Knife; (6) Tai Chi Short and Long Stick; (7) Self-Defense Applications and Mat Work.

Through Tai Chi Chuan the practitioner learns to move the body in one unit, utilizing Chi energy rather than muscle power. Without the circulation of Chi through the channels, muscles, and tendons, the Tai Chi Chuan movements are only physical exercises with little effect on the inner structure of the body. In the practice of Tai Chi Chi Kung, the increased energy flow developed through the Microcosmic Orbit, Fusion work, and Iron Shirt practice is integrated into ordinary movement, so that the body learns more efficient ways of utilizing energy in motion. Improper body movements restrict energy flow causing energy blockages, poor posture, and, in some cases, serious illness. Quite often, back problems are the result of improper posture, accumulated tension, weakened bone structure, and psychological stress.

Through Tai Chi one learns how to use one's own mass as a power to work along with the force of gravity rather than against it. A result of increased body awareness through movement is an increased awareness of one's environment and the potentials it contains. The Tai Chi practitioner may utilize the integrated

movements of the body as a means of self-defense in negative situations. Since Tai Chi is a gentle way of exercising and keeping the body fit, it can be practiced well into advanced age because the movements do not strain one's physical capacity as some aerobic exercises do.

Before beginning to study the Tai Chi Chuan form, the student must complete: (1) Opening of the Microcosmic Orbit, (2) Seminal and Ovarian Kung Fu, (3) Iron Shirt Chi Kung I, and (4) Tai Chi Chi Kung.

Tai Chi Chi Kung is divided into seven levels.

Tai Chi Chi Kung I is comprised of four parts:

a. Mind: (1) How to use one's own mass together with the force of gravity; (2) how to use the bone structure to move the whole body with very little muscular effort; and (3) how to learn and master the thirteen movements so that the mind can concentrate on directing the Chi energy.

b. Mind and Chi: Use the mind to direct the Chi flow.

c. Mind, Chi, and Earth force: How to integrate the three forces into one unit moving unimpeded through the bone structure.

d. Learn applications of Tai Chi for self-defense.

Tai Chi Chi Kung II -
Fast Form of Discharging Energy:

a. Learn how to move fast in the five directions.

b. Learn how to move the entire body structure as one piece.

c. Discharge the energy from the Earth through the body structure.

Tai Chi Chi Kung III -
Long Form Tai Chi Chuan:

a. Learn the 108 movements form.

b. Learn how to bring Chi into each movement.

c. Learn the second level of self-defense.

d. Grow "Chi eyes."

Tai Chi Chi Kung IV - the Tai Chi Sword.

Tai Chi Chi Kung V - Tai Chi Knife.

Tai Chi Chi Kung VI - Tai Chi Short and Long Stick.

Tai Chi Chi Kung VII - Application of Self-Defense and Mat Work.

Tai Chi Chuan is one of the five essential branches of the Taoist practice.

Course 6: *Taoist Five Element Nutrition; Taoist Healing Diet.*

Proper diet in tune with one's body needs, and an awareness of the seasons and the climate we live in are integral parts of the Healing Tao. It is not enough to eat healthy foods free of chemical pollutants to have good health. One has to learn the proper combination of foods according to the five tastes and the five element theory. By knowing one's predominant element, one can learn how to counteract imbalances inherent in one's nature. Also, as the seasons change, dietary needs vary. One must know how to adjust them to fit one's level of activity. Proper diet can become an instrument for maintaining health and cultivating increased levels of awareness.

INTRODUCTORY LEVEL III:
The Way of Radiant Health

Course 7: *Healing Hands Kung Fu; Awaken the Healing Hand – Five Finger Kung Fu.*

The ability to heal oneself and others is one of the five essential branches of the Healing Tao practice. Five Finger Kung Fu integrates both static and dynamic exercise forms in order to cultivate and nourish Chi which accumulates in the organs, penetrates the fasciae, tendons, and muscles, and is finally transferred out through the hands and fingers. Practitioners of body-centered therapies and various healing arts will benefit from this technique. Through the practice of Five Finger Kung Fu, you will learn how to expand your breathing capacity in order to further strengthen your internal organs, tone and

stretch the lower back and abdominal muscles, regulate weight, and connect with Father Heaven and Mother Earth healing energy; and you will learn how to develop the ability to concentrate for self-healing.

Course 8: *Chi Nei Tsang; Organ Chi Transformation Massage.*

The practice is divided into three levels: Chi Nei Tsang I, II, and III.

Chi Nei Tsang, or Organ Chi Transformation Massage, is an entire system of Chinese deep healing that works with the energy flow of the five major systems in the body: the vascular system, the lymphatic system, the nervous system, the tendon/muscle system, and the acupuncture meridian system.

In the Chi Nei Tsang practice, one is able to increase energy flow to specific organs through massaging a series of points in the navel area. In Taoist practice, it is believed that all the Chi energy and the organs, glands, brain, and nervous system are joined in the navel; therefore, energy blockages in the navel area often manifest as symptoms in other parts of the body. The abdominal cavity contains the large intestine, small intestine, liver, gall bladder, stomach, spleen, pancreas, bladder, and sex organs, as well as many lymph nodes. The aorta and vena cava divide into two branches at the navel area, descending into the legs.

Chi Nei Tsang works on the energy blockages in the navel and then follows the energy into the other parts of the body. Chi Nei Tsang is a very deep science of healing brought to the United States by Master Mantak Chia.

Course 9: *Space Dynamics; The Taoist Art of Placement.*

Feng Shui has been used by Chinese people and emperors for five thousand years. It combines ancient Chinese Geomancy, Taoist Metaphysics, dynamic Psychology, and modern Geomagnetics to diagnose energy, power, and phenomena in nature, people, and buildings. The student will gain greater awareness of his own present situation, and see more choices for freedom and growth through the interaction of the Five Elements.

INTERMEDIATE LEVEL:
Foundations of Spiritual Practice

Course 10: *Lesser Enlightenment (Kan and Li); Opening of the Twelve Channels; Raising the Soul and Developing the Energy Body.*

Lesser Enlightenment of Kan and Li (Yin and Yang Mixed): This formula is called Siaow Kan Li in Chinese, and involves a literal steaming of the sexual energy (Ching or creative) into life-force energy (Chi) in order to feed the soul or energy body. One might say that the transfer of the sexual energy power throughout the whole body and brain begins with the practice of Kan and Li. The crucial secret of this formula is to reverse the usual sites of Yin and Yang power, thereby provoking liberation of the sexual energy.

This formula includes the cultivation of the root (the Hui-Yin) and the heart center, and the transformation of sexual energy into pure Chi at the navel. This inversion places the heat of the bodily fire beneath the coolness of the bodily water. Unless this inversion takes place, the fire simply moves up and burns the body out. The water (the sexual fluid) has the tendency to flow downward and out. When it dries out, it is the end. This formula reverses normal wasting of energy by the highly advanced method of placing the water in a closed vessel (cauldron) in the body, and then cooking the sperm (sexual energy) with the fire beneath. If the water (sexual energy) is not sealed, it will flow directly into the fire and extinguish it or itself be consumed.

This formula preserves the integrity of both elements, thus allowing the steaming to go on for great periods of time. The essential formula is to never let the fire rise without having water to heat above it, and to never allow the water to spill into the fire. Thus, a warm, moist steam is produced containing tremendous energy and health benefits, to regrow all the glands, the nervous system, and the lymphatic system, and to increase pulsation.

The formula consists of:

1. Mixing the water (Yin) and fire (Yang), or male and female, to give birth to the soul;

2. Transforming the sexual power (creative force) into vital energy (Chi), gathering and purifying the Microcosmic outer alchemical agent;

3. Opening the twelve major channels;

4. Circulating the power in the solar orbit (cosmic orbit);

5. Turning back the flow of generative force to fortify the body and the brain, and restore it to its original condition before puberty;

6. Regrowing the thymus gland and lymphatic system;

7. Sublimation of the body and soul: self-intercourse. Giving birth to the immortal soul (energy body).

Course 11: *Greater Enlightenment (Kan and Li); Raising the Spirit and Developing the Spiritual Body.*

This formula comprises the Taoist Dah Kan Li (Ta Kan Li) practice. It uses the same energy relationship of Yin and Yang inversion but increases to an extraordinary degree the amount of energy that may be drawn up into the body. At this stage, the mixing, transforming, and harmonizing of energy takes place in the solar plexus. The increasing amplitude of power is due to the fact that the formula not only draws Yin and Yang energy from within the body, but also draws the power directly from Heaven and Earth or ground (Yang and Yin, respectively), and adds the elemental powers to those of one's own body. In fact, power can be drawn from any energy source, such as the Moon, wood, Earth, flowers, animals, light, etc.

The formula consists of:

1. Moving the stove and changing the cauldron;

2. Greater water and fire mixture (self-intercourse);

3. Greater transformation of sexual power into the higher level;

4. Gathering the outer and inner alchemical agents to restore the generative force and invigorate the brain;

5. Cultivating the body and soul;

6. Beginning the refining of the sexual power (generative force, vital force, Ching Chi);

7. Absorbing Mother Earth (Yin) power and Father Heaven (Yang) power. Mixing with sperm and ovary power (body), and soul;

8. Raising the soul;

9. Retaining the positive generative force (creative) force, and keeping it from draining away;

10. Gradually doing away with food, and depending on self sufficiency and universal energy;

11. Giving birth to the spirit, transferring good virtues and Chi energy channels into the spiritual body;

12. Practicing to overcome death;

13. Opening the crown;

14. Space travelling.

Course 12: *Greatest Enlightenment (Kan and Li).*

This formula is Yin and Yang power mixed at a higher energy center. It helps to reverse the aging process by re-establishing the thymus glands and increasing natural immunity. This means that healing energy is radiated from a more powerful point in the body, providing greater benefits to the physical and ethereal bodies. The formula consists of:

1. Moving the stove and changing the cauldron to the higher center;

2. Absorbing the Solar and Lunar power;

3. Greatest mixing, transforming, steaming, and purifying of sexual power (generative force), soul, Mother Earth, Father Heaven, Solar and Lunar power for gathering the Microcosmic inner alchemical agent;

4. Mixing the visual power with the vital power;

5. Mixing (sublimating) the body, soul and spirit.

ADVANCED LEVEL:
The Immortal Tao:
The Realm of Soul and Spirit

Course 13: *Sealing of the Five Senses.*

This very high formula effects a literal transmutation of the warm current or Chi into mental energy or energy of the soul. To do this, we must seal the five senses, for each one is an open gate of energy loss. In other words, power flows out from each of the sense organs unless there is an esoteric sealing of these doors of energy movement. They must release energy only when specifically called upon to convey information.

Abuse of the senses leads to far more energy loss and degradation than people ordinarily realize. Examples of misuse of the senses are as follows: if you look too much, the seminal fluid is harmed; listen too much, and the mind is harmed; speak too much, and the salivary glands are harmed; cry too much, and the blood is harmed; have sexual intercourse too often, and the marrow is harmed, etc.

Each of the elements has a corresponding sense through which its elemental force may be gathered or spent. The eye corresponds to fire; the tongue to water; the left ear to metal; the right ear to wood; the nose to Earth.

The fifth formula consists of:

1. Sealing the five thieves: ears, eyes, nose, tongue, and body;

2. Controlling the heart, and seven emotions (pleasure, anger, sorrow, joy, love, hate, and desire);

3. Uniting and transmuting the inner alchemical agent into life-preserving true vitality;

4. Purifying the spirit;

5. Raising and educating the spirit; stopping the spirit from wandering outside in quest of sense data;

6. Eliminating decayed food, depending on the undecayed food, the universal energy is the True Breatharian.

Course 14: *Congress of Heaven and Earth*

This formula is difficult to describe in words. It involves the incarnation of a male and a female entity within the body of the adept. These two entities have sexual intercourse within the body. It involves the mixing of the Yin and Yang powers on and about the crown of the head, being totally open to receive energy from above, and the regrowth of the pineal gland to its fullest use. When the pineal gland has developed to its fullest potential, it will serve as a compass to tell us in which direction our aspirations can be found. Taoist Esotericism is a method of mastering the spirit, as described in Taoist Yoga. Without the body, the Tao cannot be attained, but with the body, truth can never be realized. The practitioner of Taoism should preserve his physical body with the same care as he would a precious diamond, because it can be used as a medium to achieve immortality. If, however, you do not abandon it when you reach your destination, you will not realize the truth.

This formula consists of:

1. Mingling (uniting) the body, soul, spirit, and the universe (cosmic orbit);

2. Fully developing the positive to eradicate the negative completely;

3. Returning the spirit to nothingness.

Course 15: *Reunion of Heaven and Man*

We compare the body to a ship, and the soul to the engine and propeller of a ship. This ship carries a very precious and very large diamond which it is assigned to transport to a very distant shore. If your ship is damaged (a sick and ill body), no matter how good the engine is, you are not going to get very far and may even

sink. Thus, we advise against spiritual training unless all of the channels in the body have been properly opened, and have been made ready to receive the 10,000 or 100,000 volts of super power which will pour down into them. The Taoist approach, which has been passed down to us for over five thousand years, consists of many thousands of methods. The formulae and practices we describe in these books are based on such secret knowledge and the author's own experience during over twenty years of study and of successively teaching thousands of students.

The main goal of Taoists:

1. This level—overcoming reincarnation, and the fear of death through enlightenment;

2. Higher level—the immortal spirit and life after death;

3. Highest level—the immortal spirit in an immortal body. This body functions like a mobile home to the spirit and soul as it moves through the subtle planes, allowing greater power of manifestation.

HEALING TAO BOOKS

THE MULTI-ORGASMIC MAN

In this book co-written by Master Mantak Chia and Doug Arava, and published by Harper Collins, you'll learn the amazing facts about the multi-orgasmic capabilities of men. By learning to separate orgasm and ejaculation – two 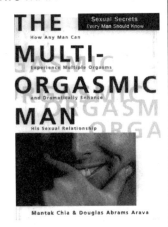 distinct physical processes – men can transform a momentary release into countless peaks of whole body orgasms without losing an erection. In addition to becoming better sexual partners, multi-orgasmic men enjoy increased vitality and longevity because they minimize the fatigue and depletion that follow ejaculation.

$20.00 plus $3.95 for postage & handling

(Foreign Shipping: Please see page 182)

Order by Item No. B13

AWAKEN HEALING LIGHT OF THE TAO

This book contains procedures that have been refined with over ten years of teaching experience at hundreds of workshops and feedback from thousands of students. Awaken Healing Light of the Tao clearly presents the most comprehensive instructions (basic and advanced) 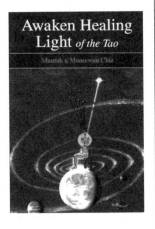 for realizing and developing our inherent energetic potentials. It explains in simple terms how to use the power of the mind to refine, transform, and guide energy through the two primary acupuncture channels of the body which comprise the Microscomic Orbit. Practical methods for strengthening the immune system, recycling stressful energies, and restoring vibrant health are included. Illustrated by Juan Li. Softbound. 640 pages.

$16.95 plus $3.95 for postage & handling

(Foreign Shipping: Please see page 182)

Order by Item No. B11

TAOIST SECRETS OF LOVE: CULTIVATING MALE SEXUAL ENERGY

Master Mantak Chia reveals for the first time to the general public the ancient sexual secrets of the Taoist sages. These methods enable men to conserve and transform sexual energy through its circulation in the Microcosmic Orbit, invigorating and rejuvenating the body's vital functions. Hidden for centuries, these esoteric techniques make the process of linking sexual energy and transcendent states of consciousness accessible to the reader.

This revolutionary book teaches: Higher Taoist practices for alchemical transmutation of body, mind, and spirit; The secret of achieving and maintaining full sexual potency; The Taoist "valley orgasm"—pathway to higher bliss; How to conserve and store sperm in the body; The exchange and balancing of male and female energies within the body, and with one's partner; How this can fuel higher achievement in career, personal power, and sports.

This book, co-authored with Michael Winn, is written clearly, and illustrated with many detailed diagrams. Softbound. 250 pages.

$14.95 plus $1.95 for postage & handling

(Foreign Shipping: Please see page 182)

Order by Item No. B02

HEALING LOVE THROUGH THE TAO: CULTIVATING FEMALE SEXUAL ENERGY

This book outlines the methods for cultivating female sexual energy. Master Mantak Chia and Maneewan Chia introduce for the first time in the West the different techniques for transforming and circulating female sexual energy. The book teaches: The Taoist internal alchemical practices to nourish body, mind, and spirit; How to eliminate energy loss through menstruation; How to reduce the length of menstruations; How to conserve and store ovary energy in the body; The exchange and balance of male and female energies within the body, and with one's partner; How to rejuvenate the body and mind through vaginal exercises.

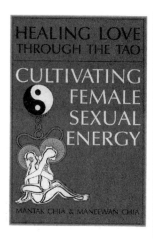

Written in clear language by Master Mantak Chia and Maneewan Chia. Published by Healing Tao Books. Softbound. 328 pages.

$14.95 plus $3.95 for postage & handling

(Foreign Shipping: Please see page 182)

Order by Item No. B06

TAOIST WAYS TO TRANSFORM STRESS INTO VITALITY

The foundations of success, personal power, health, and peak performance are created by knowing how to transform stress into vitality and power using the techniques of the Inner Smile and Six Healing Sounds, and circulating the smile energy in the Microcosmic Orbit.

The Inner Smile teaches you how to connect with your inner organs, fall in love with them, and smile to them, so that the emotions and stress can be transformed into creativity, learning, healing, and peak performance energy.

The Six Healing Sounds help to cool down the system, eliminate trapped energy, and clean the toxins out of the organs to establish organs that are in peak condition. By Master Mantak Chia. Published by Healing Tao Books. Softbound. 156 pages.

$10.95 plus $3.95 for postage & handling

(Foreign Shipping: Please see page 182)

Order by Item No. B03

CHI SELF-MASSAGE: THE TAOIST WAY OF REJUVENATION

Tao Rejuvenation uses one's internal energy or Chi to strengthen and rejuvenate the sense organs (eyes, ears, nose, tongue), the teeth, the skin, and the inner organs. The techniques are five thousand years old, and, until now, were closely guarded secrets passed on from a Master to a small group of students, with each Master only knowing a small part. For the first time the entire system has been pieced together in a logical sequence, and is presented in such a way that only five or ten minutes of practice daily will improve complexion, vision, hearing, sinuses, gums, teeth, tongue, internal organs, and general stamina. (This form of massage is very different from muscular massage.)

By Master Mantak Chia. Published by Healing Tao Books. Softbound. 176 pages.

$10.95 plus $3.95 for postage & handling

(Foreign Shipping: Please see page 182)

Order by Item No. B04

IRON SHIRT CHI KUNG I: INTERNAL ORGANS EXERCISE

The main purpose of Iron Shirt is not for fighting, but to perfect the body, to win great health, to increase performance, to fight disease, to protect the vital organs from injuries, and to lay the groundwork for higher, spiritual work. Iron Shirt I teaches how to increase the performance of the organs during sports, speech, singing, and dancing.

Learn how to increase the Chi pressure throughout the whole system by Iron Shirt Chi Kung breathing, to awaken and circulate internal energy (Chi), to transfer force through the bone structure and down to the ground. Learn how to direct the Earth's power through your bone structure, to direct the internal power to energize and strengthen the organs, and to energize and increase the Chi pressure in the fasciae (connective tissues).

By Master Mantak Chia. Published by Healing Tao Books. Softbound. 320 pages.

$14.95 plus $3.95 for postage & handling

(Foreign Shipping: Please see page 182)

Order by Item No. B05

BONE MARROW NEI KUNG: IRON SHIRT CHI KUNG III

Bone Marrow Nei Kung is a system to cultivate internal power. By absorbing cosmic energy into the bones, the bone marrow is revitalized, blood replenished, and the life-force within is nourished. These methods are known to make the body impervious to illness and disease. In ancient times, the "Steel Body" attained through this practice was a coveted asset in the fields of Chinese medicine and martial arts. Taoist methods of "regrowing" the bone marrow are crucial to rejuvenating the body, which in turn rejuvenates the mind and spirit. This system has not been revealed before, but in this ground-breaking work Master Chia divulges the step-by-step practice of his predecessors.

By Master Mantak Chia and Maneewan Chia. Published by Healing Tao Books. Softbound. 288 pages.

$14.95 plus $3.95 for postage & handling

(Foreign Shipping: Please see page 182)

Order by Item No. B08

FUSION of the FIVE ELEMENTS I

Fusion of the Five Elements I, first in the Taoist Inner Alchemy Series, offers basic and advanced meditations for transforming negative emotions. Based on the Taoist Five Element Theory regarding the five elemental forces of the universe, the student learns how to control negative energies and how to transform them into useful energy. The student also learns how to create a pearl of radiant energy and how to increase its power with additional internal energy (virtue energy) as well as external sources of energy—Universal, Cosmic Particle, and Earth. All combine in a balanced way to prepare the pearl for its use in the creation of an energy body. The creation of the energy body is the next major step in achieving the goal of creating an immortal spirit. Master Mantak Chia leads you, step by step, into becoming an emotionally balanced, controlled, and stronger individual as he offers you the key to a spiritual independence.

$12.95 plus $3.95 for postage & handling

(Foreign Shipping: Please see page 182)

Order by Item No. B09

CHI NEI TSANG (Internal Organ Chi Massage)

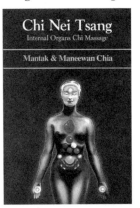

Chi Nei Tsang presents a whole new understanding and approach to healing with detailed explanations of self-healing techniques and methods of teaching others to heal themselves. Also included are ways to avoid absorbing negative, sick energies from others.

The navel's center is where negative emotions, stress, tension, and sickness accumulate and congest. When this occurs, all vital functions stagnate. Using Chi Nei Tsang techniques in and around the area of the navel provides the fastest method of healing and the most permanent results.

By Master Mantak Chia and Maneewan Chia. Published by Healing Tao Books. Softbound. 448 pages.

$16.95 plus $3.95 for postage & handling

(Foreign Shipping: Please see page 182)

Order by Item No. B10

AWAKEN HEALING ENERGY THROUGH the TAO

Learn how to strengthen your internal organs and increase circulation through the flow of Chi energy. Included are precise instructions for practice, and detailed illustrations of energy centers, organs, and anatomical structures as well as descriptions of the higher levels of the Taoist meditation system. By Master Mantak Chia. Softbound. 193 pages.

$12.50 plus $3.95 for postage & handling

(Foreign Shipping: Please see page 182)

Order by Item No. B01

INSTRUCTORS' BOOKS

LIVING in the TAO by THE PROFESSOR

This is a Healing Tao instructor's accumulation of knowledge and wisdom from a volume of books and life experiences attained through his practice and instruction. An insider's view of the Tao.

$9.95 plus $3.95 for postage & handling

(Foreign Shipping: Please see page 182)

Order by Item No. IB01

THE TAO AND THE TREE OF LIFE

Using the basic structure of the Shamanic Universe, this book provides a context in which to examine the concepts, philosophy, and practical work of Taoist Internal Alchemy. Revealing parallels between Hebrew and western traditions, and long-lost sexual and alchemical secrets, hidden in the Zohar and Sepher Yetzirah.

$14.95 plus $3.95 for postage & handling
(Foreign Shipping: Please see page 182)
Order by Item No. IB02

THE TAO OF NATURAL BREATHING
by Dennis Lewis

$17.95 plus $3.95 for postage & handling
(Foreign Shipping: Please see page 182)
Order by Item No. IB03

ANGEL'S HEART:
POETRY AND THEMES OF THE TAO

$9.95 plus $3.95 for postage & handling
(Foreign Shipping: Please see page 182)
Order by Item No. IB04

FORTH COMING PUBLICATIONS

COSMIC CHI KUNG

Techniques developing healing hands and ability to heal from a distance.

FIVE ELEMENT NUTRITION

Ancient Chinese cooking based on the Five Elements Theory.

FUSION OF THE FIVE ELEMENTS II

Thrusting and Belt Channels. Growing positive emotions, psychic and emotional self-defense.

COSMIC COMIC BOOKS

Join us for some enlightened humor. Our first theme comic book. $5.95, add $3.95 for shipping and handling. **CB01**: The Inner Smile (Energy Medicine of the Future)

AUDIO & VIDEO TAPES

VHS VIDEO

Invite Master Chia into your living room.

Guided videos 30-60 minutes long $29.95 per tape. Please order by Item Number. Our videos are available in PAL System. Add postage and handling as follows: 1 video - $3.95, 2 videos - $5.75, 3 or more videos - $6.50.
(Foreign Shipping: Please see page 182)

Item	Title
V40-G	Home Basic Sitting Meditation (complements V61)
V41-G	Home Basic Standing Meditation
V42-G	Inner Smile
V43-G	Six Healing Sounds

Workshop videos 60-120 minutes long, one tape $39.95; 2 tapes set $69.95.

Item	Title
V50-TP	Tai Chi Chi Kung I (set of 2 tapes)
V51-TP	Tai Chi Chi Kung II (set of 2 tapes)
V52-TP	Chi Self Massage
V57-TP	Iron Shirt Chi Kung I
V58- TP	Iron Shirt III—Bone Marrow Nei Kung (2 tapes)
V59- TP	Iron Shirt II—Tendons exercises (set of 2 tapes)
V60-TP	Cosmic Chi Kung (Basic and Advanced Buddha Palm)
V61-TM	Awaken Healing Light (set of 2 tapes)
V63-TP	Healing Love through The Tao (set of 2 tapes)
V64-TM	Fusion of Five Elements I (set of 2 tapes)
V65-TM	Fusion of Five Elements II (set of 2 tapes)
V66-TM	Fusion of Five Elements III (set of 2 tapes)
V67-TP	Chi Nei Tsang (set of 2 tapes)
V68-P	Chi Nei Tsang's Healing Power Practice
V69-TP	Tao-In: Regaining a Youthful Body (set of 2 tapes) New in 1995

CASSETTE TAPES

Guided Practice Tapes C09-C18 are guided by Master Mantak Chia. $9.95 each, add $3.95 for shipping and handling.
(Foreign Shipping: Please see page 182)

Item	Title
C09	Inner Smile
C10	Six Healing Sounds
C11	Microcosmic Orbit
C11a	Healing Love
C12	Tai Chi Chi Kung I
C13	Iron Shirt Chi Kung I
C14	Sitting Meditation for Home Instruction
C15	Standing Meditation for Home Instruction
C16	Fusion of the Five Elements I
C17	Fusion of the Five Elements II
C18	Fusion of the Five Elements III

Weekend Workshops

Taught by Master Mantak Chia. Only limited quantities. $30 each set, add $5.95 for shipping and handling.

Item	Title	Tapes/set
C20	Tai Chi Chi Kung I	4
C21	Iron Shirt Chi Kung I	4
C23	Iron Shirt Chi Kung III	4
C24	Fusion of the Five Elements I	4
C25	Fusion of the Five Elements II	4
C26	Fusion of the Five Elements III	4

CARDS, POSTERS & CHARTS . . .

BONE MARROW NEI KUNG
(IRON SHIRT III) EQUIPMENT

Only sold as listed!

(Foreign Shipping: Please see page 182)

Item	Title	Price	P&H
62C	Untreated Drilled Jade Egg	$15.95	$3.95
62DG	Chi Weight-Lifting Bar and Silk Cloth	25.95	7.25
62EF	Wire Hitter, Rattan Hitter, Bag for Equipment	39.95	7.25

CARDS

• Eight Immortal Greeting cards sold in sets of 2 (16 cards in all). Full color, depicting the Eight Immortals with a short history of each one. Ideal for sharing with family and friends!

• Instructional formulas Chi Cards. Now also available in French.

Item	Title	Cards per set
GC01	Eight Immortal Greeting Cards Set	
CC01	Chi Cards - Level 1	20
CC02	Chi Cards - Level 2	18
CC03	Chi Cards - Level 3	18
CC04	Chi Cards - Level 4	25

$9.95 each, add $3.95 for shipping and handling.

POSTERS

18 x 22", four-color process posters were created by artist Juan Li. $7.50 each, add $3.95 for shipping and handling. Please order by item number.

Healing Tao System Posters

Sold as set of 8-9 for $59.95

Item No. 45.

The Microcosmic Orbit – Small Heavenly Cycle – The Governor Channel (Yang)

The Governor Channel of the Microcosmic Orbit Meditation allows the Yang (hot) energy to flow from the base of the spine to the brain.

Item No. P32

Healing Love and Sex – Ovarian Kung Fu

The Taoists teach women to regulate their menstrual flow and transmute sexual orgasm into higher spiritual love. The techniques of Seminal and Ovarian Kung Fu allow the practitioner to harness sexual impulses so that sex does not control the person. By controlling sexual impulses, people are able to move from the mortal level into higher levels of consciousness.

Item No. P36

Fusion of the Five Elements II

Enhancing and Strengthening the Virtues. Fusion of the Five Elements II strengthens positive emotions, balances the organs, and encourages in men and women the natural virtues of gentleness, kindness, respect, honor, and righteousness.

Item No. P38

Fusion of the Five Elements II

Thrusting Channels. Running through the center of the body, the Thrusting Routes allow the absorption of cosmic energies for greater radiance and power.

Item No. P39

Fusion of the Five Elements II

Nine Belt Channel. The Taoist Belt Channel spins a web of Chi around the major energy vortexes in the body, protecting the psyche by connecting the power of Heaven and Earth.

Item No. P40

The Harmony of Yin and Yang

"Yin cannot function without the help of Yang; Yang cannot function without the help of Yin."
—Taoist Canon, 8th century A.D.

Item No. P41

Pa Kua: The Cauldron of Fusing the Energy and Emotions.

Also sold separately, $7.50 each copy, add $3.95 for shipping and handling
Item No. P42

Fusion of the Five Elements III – Yin Bridge and Regulator Channels.

Fusion of the Five Elements III uses special meridians to cleanse the aura and regulate high-voltage energy absorbed by the body during meditation.

Item No. P43

Fusion of the Five Elements III – Yang Bridge and Regulator Channels.

Fusion of the Five Elements III teaches the yogic secrets of safely regulating the release of the kundalini power using special meridians.

Item No. P44

CHARTS

Body/Mind/Spirit Chart

23" x 35", full-color chart by Susan McKay.

Item No. CH47
$7.50 per copy plus $3.95 for postage and handling

The Inner Alchemy of the Tao

Beautifully illustrated chart. Instructional pamphlet is included.

Item No. CH48

The Eight Immortal Forces

The legendary figures of the Eight Immortals are depicted in this chart with full explanations of their mysteries. Instructional pamphlet is included.

Item No. CH49
$9.50 per copy plus, $3.95 shipping and handling.

THE INTERNATIONAL HEALING TAO CENTERS

For further information about any of our courses or centers, or to order books, posters, etc., please write or call:

The Healing Tao Center
Order Fulfillment
400 Keystone Industrial Park
Dunmore, PA 18512
Tel: (717) 348-4310
Fax: (717) 348-4313

There are also Healing Tao Centers in:

America:
Bermuda

Canada:
Ontario, British Columbia, Quebec

United States:
Alabama, Arizona
California
  Los Angeles
  San Francisco
Colorado, Connecticut, Delaware, Florida, Hawaii, Illinois, Kansas, Massachusetts, Michigan, Minnesota, New Hampshire, New Jersey, New Mexico, New York, North Carolina, Oklahoma, Oregon, Pennsylvania, South Dakota, Virginia

Asia
India, Japan, Thailand

Australia

Europe
Austria, England, France, Germany, Greece, Holland, Italy, Netherlands, Spain, Switzerland

Our new center in Thailand holds retreats during the winter and summer seasons, and is located in Chiang Mai. For more information, please call, fax, or write to:

The Healing Tao Center at Tao Garden
274 Moo 7, Laung Nua
Doi Saket, Chiang Mai 50220
Phone: (66, 53) 495-596 through 599
Fax: (66, 53) 495-852

HOW TO ORDER

Prices and Taxes:

Subject to change without notice. New York State residents please add 8.25% sales tax.

Payment: Send personal check, money order, certified check, or bank cashier's check to:

THE HEALING TAO CENTER – Order Fulfillment

400 Keystone Industrial Park
Dunmore, PA 18512
Tel. (717) 348-4310 • FAX: (717) 348-4313

All foreign checks must be drawn on a U.S. bank.

We also accept:

Shipping:

Domestic Shipping

Via UPS, requires a complete street address. Allow 3-4 weeks for delivery.

Order Total	Domestic Zones 1-6	Domestic Zones 7&8
$20.00 or less	$3.95	$3.95
20.01 – 40.00	6.95	7.25
40.01 – 60.00	8.50	9.25
60.01 – 80.00	9.75	10.75
80.01 – 100.00	11.00	12.75
100.01 – 120.00	12.25	14.50
120.01 – 140.00	13.50	16.25
140.01 – 200.00	16.50	21.50
Over 200.00	add $4.95 for every $50.00	

Zones 7&8 are zip codes with the first 3 digits:
577, 586 - 593, 677 - 679, 690, 693, 733, 739, 763 - 772, 774 - 774, 778 - 797, 798 - 799, 800 - 899, 900 - 994

All other Zip codes are Zones 1 - 6

Foreign Shipping

Via Worldmail by DHL, surface mail ($7.95 per book), air mail ($15.95 per book). Courier service by air, as an alternative for traceable shipments or heavy orders, is also available as a collect service. For other products please see chart below.

Order Total	Foreign by Surface	Foreign by Air
$20.00 or less	$7.95	$15.95
20.01 – 40.00	17.95	30.95
40.01 – 60.00	27.50	45.95
60.01 – 80.00	37.95	60.95
80.01 – 100.00	47.95	75.95
100.01 – 120.00	57.95	90.95
120.01 – 140.00	67.95	105.95
140.01 – 200.00	97.95	150.95
Over 200.00	add $20.95 for every $50	add 40.95 for every $50

Please call or write for additional information in your area.